Christmas
1987

From the Editors of
Better Homes and Gardens® Books

A joyous celebration of the Christmas season, *Christmas 1987* will delight you with holiday stories, foods, customs, crafts, and activities.

TABLE OF CONTENTS

CELEBRATING THE SEASON

PRESERVING THE HERITAGE

GATHERING
THE
FAMILY

SHARING
THE
SPIRIT

CELEBRATING
THE
SEASON

He comes—the brave old Christmas!
His sturdy steps I hear;
We will give him a hearty welcome,
For he comes but once a year!

—*19th-century English verse*

The Peterkins' Christmas-Tree

—Lucretia P. Hale

Early in the autumn the Peterkins began to prepare for their Christmas-tree. Everything was done in great privacy, as it was to be a surprise to the neighbors, as well as to the rest of the family. Mr. Peterkin had been up to Mr. Bromwick's wood-lot, and with his consent, selected the tree. Agamemnon went to look at it occasionally after dark, and Solomon John made frequent visits to it mornings, just after sunrise. Mr. Peterkin drove Elizabeth Eliza and her mother that way, and pointed furtively to it with his whip; but none of them ever spoke of it aloud to each other. It was suspected that the little boys had been to see it Wednesday and Saturday afternoons. But they came home with their pockets full of chestnuts, and said nothing about it.

At length Mr. Peterkin had it cut down and brought secretly into the Larkins' barn. A week or two before Christmas a measurement was made of it with Elizabeth Eliza's yard-measure. To Mr. Peterkin's great dismay it was discovered that it was too high to stand in the back parlor.

This fact was brought out at a secret council of Mr. and Mrs. Peterkin, Elizabeth Eliza, and Agamemnon.

Agamemnon suggested that it might be set up slanting; but Mrs. Peterkin was very sure it would make her dizzy, and the candles would drip.

But a brilliant idea came to Mr. Peterkin. He proposed that the ceiling of the parlor should be raised to make room for the top of the tree.

Elizabeth Eliza thought the space would need to be quite large. It must not be like a small box, or you could not see the tree.

"Yes," said Mr. Peterkin, "I should have the ceiling lifted all across the room; the effect would be finer."

Elizabeth Eliza objected to having the whole ceiling raised, because her room was over the back parlor, and she would have no floor while the alteration was going on, which would be very awkward. Besides, her room was not very high now, and, if the floor were raised, perhaps she could not walk in it upright.

Mr. Peterkin explained that he didn't propose altering the whole ceiling, but to lift up a ridge across the room at the back part where the tree was to stand. This would make a hump, to be sure, in Elizabeth Eliza's room; but it would go across the whole room.

Elizabeth Eliza said she would not mind that. It would be like the cuddy thing that comes up on the deck of a ship, that you sit against, only here you would not have the sea-sickness. She thought she should like it, for a rarity. She might use it for a divan.

Mrs. Peterkin thought it would come in the worn place of the carpet, and might be a convenience in making the carpet over.

Agamemnon was afraid there would be trouble in keeping the matter secret, for it would be a long piece of work for a carpenter; but Mr. Peterkin proposed having the carpenter for a day or two, for a number of other jobs.

One of them was to make all the chairs in the house of the same height, for Mrs. Peterkin had nearly broken her spine by sitting down in a chair that she had supposed was her own rocking-chair, and it had proved to be two inches lower. The little boys were now large enough to sit in any chair; so a medium was fixed upon to satisfy all the family, and the chairs were made uniformly of the same height.

On consulting the carpenter, however, he insisted that the tree could be cut off at the lower end to suit the height of the parlor, and demurred at so great a change as altering the ceiling. But Mr. Peterkin had set his mind upon the improvement, and Elizabeth Eliza had cut her carpet in preparation for it.

So the folding-doors into the back parlor were closed, and for nearly a fortnight before Christ-

mas there was great litter of fallen plastering, and laths, and chips, and shavings; and Elizabeth Eliza's carpet was taken up, and the furniture had to be changed, and one night she had to sleep at the Bromwicks', for there was a long hole in her floor that might be dangerous.

All this delighted the little boys. They could not understand what was going on. Perhaps they suspected a Christmas-tree, but they did not know why a Christmas-tree should have so many chips, and were still more astonished at the hump that appeared in Elizabeth Eliza's room. It must be a Christmas present, or else the tree in a box.

Some aunts and uncles, too, arrived a day or two before Christmas, with some small cousins. These cousins occupied the attention of the little boys, and there was a great deal of whispering

and mystery, behind doors, and under the stairs, and in the corners of the entry.

Solomon John was busy, privately making some candles for the tree. He had been collecting some bayberries, as he understood they made very nice candles, so that it would not be necessary to buy any.

The elders of the family never all went into the back parlor together, and all tried not to see what was going on. Mrs. Peterkin would go in with Solomon John, or Mr. Peterkin with Elizabeth Eliza, or Elizabeth Eliza and Agamemnon and Solomon John. The little boys and the small cousins were never allowed even to look inside the room.

Elizabeth Eliza meanwhile went into town a number of times. She wanted to consult Amanda as to how much ice-cream they should need, and

continued

whether they could make it at home, as they had cream and ice. She was pretty busy in her own room; the furniture had to be changed, and the carpet altered. The "hump" was higher than she expected. There was danger of bumping her own head whenever she crossed it. She had to nail some padding on the ceiling for fear of accidents.

The afternoon before Christmas, Elizabeth Eliza, Solomon John, and their father collected in the back parlor for a council. The carpenters had done their work, and the tree stood at its full height at the back of the room, the top stretching up into the space arranged for it. All the chips and shavings were cleared away, and it stood on a neat box.

But what were they to put upon the tree?

Solomon John had brought in his supply of candles; but they proved to be very "stringy" and very few of them. It was strange how many bayberries it took to make a few candles! The little boys had helped him, and he had gathered as much as a bushel of bayberries. He had put them in water, and skimmed off the wax, according to the directions; but there was so little wax!

Solomon John had given the little boys some of the bits sawed off from the legs of the chairs. He had suggested that they should cover them with gilt paper, to answer for gilt apples, without telling them what they were for.

These apples, a little blunt at the end, and the candles, were all they had for the tree!

After all her trips into town Elizabeth Eliza had forgotten to bring anything for it.

"I thought of candies and sugar-plums," she said; "but I concluded if we made caramels ourselves we should not need them. But, then, we have not made caramels. The fact is, that day my head was full of my carpet. I had bumped it pretty badly, too."

Mr. Peterkin wished he had taken, instead of a fir-tree, an apple-tree he had seen in October, full of red fruit.

"But the leaves would have fallen off by this time," said Elizabeth Eliza.

"And the apples, too," said Solomon John.

"It is odd I should have forgotten, that day I went in on purpose to get the things," said Elizabeth Eliza, musingly. "But I went from shop to shop, and didn't know exactly what to get. I saw a great many gilt things for Christmas-trees; but I knew the little boys were making the gilt apples; there were plenty of candles in the shops, but I knew Solomon John was making the candles."

Mr. Peterkin thought it was quite natural.

Solomon John wondered if it were too late for them to go into town now.

Elizabeth Eliza could not go in the next morning, for there was to be a grand Christmas dinner, and Mr. Peterkin could not be spared, and Solomon John was sure he and Agamemnon would not know what to buy. Besides, they would want to try the candles to-night.

Mr. Peterkin asked if the presents everybody had been preparing would not answer. But Elizabeth Eliza knew they would be too heavy.

A gloom came over the room. There was only a flickering gleam from one of Solomon John's candles that he had lighted by way of trial.

Solomon John again proposed going into town. He lighted a match to examine the newspaper about the trains. There were plenty of trains coming out at that hour, but none going in except a very late one. That would not leave time to do anything and come back.

"We could go in, Elizabeth Eliza and I," said Solomon John, "but we should not have time to buy anything."

Agamemnon was summoned in. Mrs. Peterkin was entertaining the uncles and aunts in the front parlor. Agamemnon wished there was time to study up something about electric lights. If they could only have a calcium light! Solomon John's candle sputtered and went out.

At this moment there was a loud knocking at the front door. The little boys, and the small cousins, and the uncles and aunts, and Mrs. Peterkin, hastened to see what was the matter.

The uncles and aunts thought somebody's house must be on fire. The door was opened, and there was a man, white with flakes, for it was beginning to snow, and he was pulling in a large box.

Mrs. Peterkin supposed it contained some of Elizabeth Eliza's purchases, so she ordered it to be pushed into the back parlor, and hastily called back her guests and the little boys into the other room. The little boys and the small cousins were sure they had seen Santa Claus himself.

Mr. Peterkin lighted the gas. The box was addressed to Elizabeth Eliza. It was from the lady from Philadelphia! She had gathered a hint from Elizabeth Eliza's letters that there was to be a Christmas-tree, and had filled this box with all that would be needed.

It was opened directly. There was every kind of gilt hanging-thing, from gilt pea-pods to butterflies on springs. There were shining flags and lanterns, and bird-cages, and nests with birds sitting on them, baskets of fruit, gilt apples and bunches of grapes, and, at the bottom of the whole, a large box of candles and a box of Philadelphia bon-bons!

Elizabeth Eliza and Solomon John could scarcely keep from screaming. The little boys and the small cousins knocked on the folding-doors to ask what was the matter.

Hastily Mr. Peterkin and the rest took out the things and hung them on the tree, and put on the candles.

When it was all done, it looked so well that Mr. Peterkin exclaimed:—

"Let us light the candles now, and send to invite all the neighbors to-night, and have the tree on Christmas Eve!"

And so it was the Peterkins had their Christmas-tree the day before, and on Christmas night could go and visit their neighbors. ♣

Perfect Projects
For Christmas Bazaars

Make your bazaar booth the most popular—and profitable—this year by stocking up on the quick-to-make best-sellers shown here and on the next few pages. Don't forget to set aside a few of these items for your own last-minute gift exchanges, too.

MATERIALS
9 cups flour
4½ cups salt
4½ cups water
Cloves; butter
Round pizza pan
Rolling pin; knife
Glossy polyurethane varnish

INSTRUCTIONS
Mix ingredients in a large bowl; knead until dough is firm. Dough should not be too dry or too moist.

Using a large pizza pan, make a doughnut-shape ring of dough 3½ inches wide and ¾ inch thick for a 10- or 14-inch wreath (for small wreaths, see below). The hole in center of ring should be slightly larger than 4 or 5 inches, depending on size of candle to be inserted in the middle of it. The dough expands slightly during baking, so the diameter of the center hole will shrink. Be sure to allow for this when fitting for the candle.

Roll out a portion of dough to ⅛-inch thickness. Cut leaves about 2½ inches wide and 3 inches long. Fringe the edges by slashing the outer edges of the wreath, overlapping the leaves all around. Scatter leaves along the top, if desired.

Make fruit by forming dough balls into pears, apples, oranges, plums, and grape clusters. Shapes should be smooth and free of cracks. Attach fruit to the wreath with water; place larger fruits on inside; smaller ones on outside. Leave portions of leaves exposed.

Press whole cloves into the fruit at angles to create stems. Remove beads from clove heads to create stars at bottoms of fruits.

Bake wreath at 200° for 18 hours. After 8 to 10 hours, or when wreath seems hard, remove it from pan and place it directly on oven rack to speed drying. *Note:* Don't turn oven to a temperature higher than 200°. Wreaths should dry rather than cook.

To achieve a toasted effect, place wreath under the broiler (not too close) and broil until lightly toasted. Since the wreath browns unevenly, use foil to cover areas that darken quickly and let rest of wreath "catch up." When wreath is hard, remove it from the oven. Melt ¼ cup butter and brush the entire top.

Allow the wreath to cool; coat with glossy polyurethane varnish.

For small wreaths (7 inches in diameter): Use 2 cups flour, 1 cup salt, and 1 cup water. Shape wreath into a doughnut 2 inches wide and ¾ inch thick. Cut leaves and shape fruit as for larger wreath, but bake for only 10 to 12 hours at 200°.

Quilt-Pattern Wreath

MATERIALS
Red and green fabric scraps
18-inch square of quilt batting
18-inch square of backing fabric
Thread
Cardboard
Quilt-maker's transfer pen

INSTRUCTIONS
To make a template, trace the full-size pattern, *below,* onto cardboard; cut out. On green fabric scraps, draw around template to make 36 hexagons, leaving ½ inch

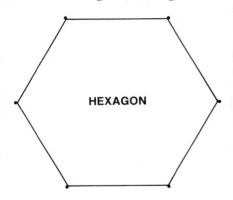

HEXAGON

between all hexagons. Mark dots on hexagons as shown on pattern. On red scraps, mark 18 hexagons. Cut out all hexagons, adding ¼-inch seam allowances on all sides.

Using ¼-inch seam allowances, join 12 green hexagons in a circle, sewing seams from dot to dot; finger-press seams open. Sew red hexagons around green hexagon circle; sew remaining green hexagons around outside of wreath.

Quilt batting to back of wreath by sewing small running stitches ⅛ inch from seams inside each hexagon. With right sides facing, sew wreath and backing together around perimeter. Clip seams; turn. Cut cardboard to fit inside wreath; insert and sew wreath closed around inside edge.

Log Carrier

MATERIALS
22x32-inch piece of 10-ounce cotton canvas
96-inch length of 1½-inch-wide heavy twill tape (available at awning repair shops)
Scrap of green calico fabric
Cookie cutter
Thread

INSTRUCTIONS
To finish the edges of the canvas, hem it all the way around, using 1-inch hems.

To make the handles, sew twill tape 5 inches from the long edges of the canvas. Place the tape ends at the center of the canvas and loop the tape around at each end, forming a handle.

To make the appliqué, use a cookie cutter as a pattern. Trace around the cookie cutter on a scrap of fabric. Cut out the appliqué and machine-stitch it to the carrier, using a zigzag stitch.

Holiday Guest Towels

MATERIALS

11x18-inch red and white guest towels

Small pieces of solid-color fabrics in the following colors: white, red, green, flesh, and black

Small pieces of red and green printed fabrics, including small-scale red-and-white striped fabric

Fusible webbing

½-inch-wide red grosgrain ribbon

½-inch-diameter white pom-pom

INSTRUCTIONS

Preshrink the towels and fabrics. Enlarge the patterns, *right,* and cut out all pattern pieces from brown paper. Referring to the photograph, cut out the fabric pieces. Cut a piece of fusible webbing to match each fabric piece.

Pin fabric and fusible webbing pieces to towel for each design as follows: Candle: candle, holly leaves, flame A, flame B, and flame C. Stocking: candy cane, two holly leaves in stocking, stocking, cuff, holly leaf on cuff, heel, and toe. Santa: face, eyes, beard, hat, hat band, holly leaves, mustache, and nose.

Note: For the stocking, the cuff overlaps the stocking top ¼ inch. For the Santa, the hat band overlaps the hat bottom and top of face ¼ inch, and the mustache overlaps the bottom of the face and top of beard ¼ inch.

Following manufacturer's directions, fuse pieces in place. Machine-appliqué pieces to towels using satin stitches. Stitch ribbons in place and tie into bows; trim ends. Stitch pom-pom in place; embroider Santa's eyebrows.

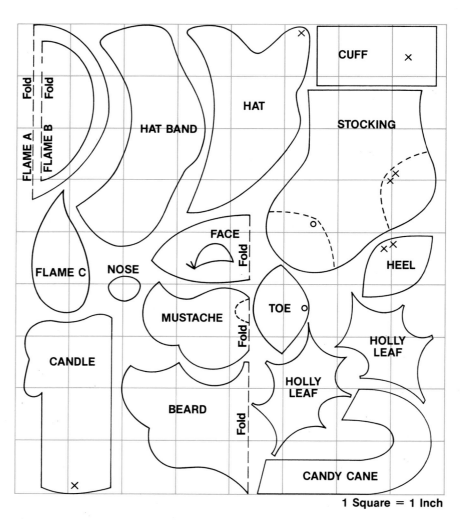

1 Square = 1 Inch

Heart
Picture Frame

MATERIALS
¼ yard of printed material
12 inches each of hardboard,
  heavy iron-on interfacing,
  and glass
5¾x4¾-inch hardboard
2 nylon tape fasteners
Thread
Water-erasable marking pen

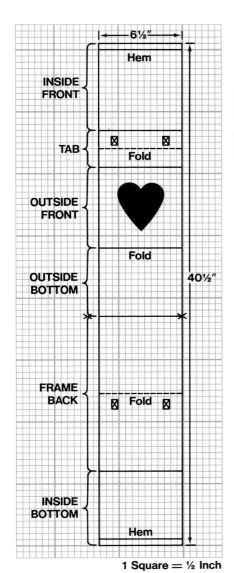

1 Square = ½ Inch

INSTRUCTIONS

Cut the fabric into a 6½x40½-inch strip. Fold the short ends under ½ inch and hem along each raw edge. Cut a 5½x6-inch facing for the heart.

To establish the picture fastening tab, picture front, bottom, and back, mark a strip along the lines indicated on the pattern, *left.* On the wrong side of the heart area, iron the interfacing.

Pin the facing over the heart area and draw a heart to fit the picture. Sew over the heart outline; trim away inside of the heart up to ¼ inch of the seam. Clip the seams around the curves, then turn the facing toward the wrong side; press.

With right sides facing, fold the strip along the fold lines so that the hemmed ends meet at Xs. Using ¼-inch seams, sew the sides of the strip together, rounding corners on the tab. Turn the frame right side out through the opening between the Xs; press.

Insert a large piece of hardboard in the picture back; sew over marked line to enclose hardboard. Sew over the marked line for the picture tab. Insert small hardboard in the short pocket; insert picture and glass inside picture front. Hand-sew fasteners to the tab and back, matching them. To set up the frame, fasten the tabs together.

Elves' Holiday Workshop

When you hold a workshop to create your very own
Christmas gifts and decorations, you'll make Santa
beam with pride. Dig out all your paints and paper,
invite your friends, and follow these suggestions—
delivered straight from the North Pole!

MATERIALS

Wood scraps
Adhesive-backed foam (such as Dr. Scholl's, available at drugstores)
Disposable pie plate
Canvas and muslin scraps
Polyester fiberfill
¼-inch cording; string
Water-base block printing ink
Fabric paints; brushes
Brayers; white glue
Pencils; crayons; paper

INSTRUCTIONS

The first step in your workshop is to create your own designs. On paper, draw simple shapes and outlines. You might draw winter animals, such as reindeer, rabbits, and birds, whose tracks can be seen in the snow. Or, draw shapes like stars or trees.

To make printing blocks, use scraps of wood that are slightly larger than the shapes you want to print. Using your drawings as patterns, cut the shapes from adhesive-backed foam. Next, remove the protective coatings from the backs of the cut foam pieces; affix them to the wood blocks. To make string-covered blocks for the geometric prints, wrap string around the blocks. Then, use glue to attach the ends of the string to the blocks. Or, cut off short pieces of string and arrange them on one side of each block.

Before you start to print, be sure to cover your worktable with newspaper. Now practice printing on fabric scraps by doing the following: Put a few spoonfuls of paint on a pie plate, roll a brayer in the paint, and apply the paint to your foam- or string-covered block. (If it's easier, you also can apply the paint to the printing surface with a brush.) Press the wood block firmly onto your paper or fabric, transferring the design onto the printing surface.

Carefully lift the block away from the surface; don't drag it or you might smear the paint. Repeat or alternate the prints to make a variety of patterns. When you're done, clean your supplies with water.

WRAPPING PAPER: Apply block prints to paper. Hang the just-printed paper to dry on an indoor clothesline. Cut gift tags from colored mat board and print them, too.

TREE TRIMS: Print onto unbleached muslin, spacing the prints 4 inches apart. When they're dry, cut around them, leaving 1½-inch borders on all sides. Cut the backs from plain muslin to match the fronts.

Ask an adult or older brother or sister to stitch the backs to the fronts ½ inch from the edges, right sides facing. Leave openings for turning. Now turn the ornaments right side out and stuff them lightly with fiberfill; slip-stitch them closed.

PILLOWS AND BAGS: Apply prints to 20x26-inch canvas rectangles. Apply the prints to the fronts; iron design to heat-set the paint. With help from an adult, sew the short ends of the rectangles together, right sides facing, to form the center back seam. Press the seam open and center it on the back side. Sew a ½-inch seam on the lower edge to form the bag bottom. Stitch a 2-inch vertical buttonhole 1½ inches below the raw edge at the top of the center front. Turn the bag top over 2 inches to form a drawstring casing; press. Stitch in place along the raw edge; thread a 1½-yard length of ¼-inch cord through the casing to form a tie. Stuff the pillow firmly with fiberfill. Sew rope ties at the tops.

Planning a Christmas Bazaar

Holiday bazaars usually fall into two different categories: the personal sales held at home with friends supplying their homemade crafts, and the large sales, often used as fund-raisers for churches or schools. Whichever type of sale you're planning, the following suggestions will help you hold a blue-ribbon bazaar destined to make its mark in your community.

Bazaars with a Personal Touch

The success of a home bazaar depends largely on how well the event is organized and publicized. Divide the responsibilities among your partners, assigning duties for bookkeeping, publicity, and the like.

Make sure that the space for the bazaar is open enough to allow guests to come and go smoothly. But confine the sales space to two or three rooms—you'll need other rooms for privacy and storage. Plan to block off the rest of the house with tables or garlands so people won't wander through.

Consider how the bazaar may affect normal family routine and traffic flow—both inside and outside the house. Be sure to invite all the neighbors, and warn them that there may be lots of parked cars during the bazaar. If necessary, have an extra person on duty to direct traffic.

Pricing properly
Plan to offer items in a variety of price ranges. If all the items are about the same price, you'll exclude a segment of potential customers who have a spending limit

in mind. It's a good idea to survey your friends and relatives on the prices you should charge—*after* you've figured how much you need to make to cover your time and materials.

Setting the date
Timing is crucial. If you hold your bazaar too early in the season, customers will just be starting their Christmas shopping—and they may be reluctant to buy before they've had a chance to shop around. Setting a date too late, though, may interfere with other holiday activities. Usually, a date around Thanksgiving will catch people at the height of the holiday spirit.

If your bazaar becomes an annual event, hold it at the same time each year so that customers will set the day aside.

Following the rules
Check with authorities to make certain that selling merchandise out of your home won't violate any local ordinances. Also check on the following:
● Contact your local revenue office to see whether you need to charge sales tax.
● Consider taking out one-day insurance to guard against theft or other possible losses.
● Make sure your driveway and sidewalks will be free of ice and snow and that all other hazards will be removed. Check on the terms of your liability coverage.
● Contact local health authorities for laws on selling food.
● Set up a system to keep accurate tax records.

Promoting yourself
To let people know of your upcoming bazaar, begin with a mailing list made up of the names and addresses of friends and relatives.

Put up signs at grocery stores, take out an ad in the newspaper, and spread the word at church and at meetings. Set your bazaar apart from others by thinking of special promotional techniques, too, such as sending out cards with coupons for, say, 10 percent off any purchase over $25.

Handling the big day
Mark off the following items from your checklist before you open the door to your customers.
● Make sure all merchandise has a clearly marked price tag. Anything that's not for sale should be removed from the display area.
● Serve coffee or tea to encourage leisurely browsing.
● Print copies of a card with the names and phone numbers of all the crafters. This will give customers one easy reference if they want to call for more orders.
● Hand out blank shopping lists so customers can take notes as they browse, keeping track of what they might buy for each person on their gift list.
● Assign all partners a code number to place on their price tags. For each purchase, make out sales slips in duplicate and include the code number so you can total each person's earnings at day's end.
● Be sure there's someone in each room to keep an eye on customers and answer any questions.
● Ask customers to sign a guest book, then add these names to your mailing list next year.
continued

Big-Scale Bazaars

Bazaars on a grand scale require detailed planning long before Christmas. In fact, as soon as New Year's is over, it's time to form a steering committee and begin your plans.

The steering committee should be composed of the chairpersons for various tasks: dealer contact, publicity, logistics, food, decorating, and other areas. These committee chairpersons should then gather their own committees of helpers.

Ask each group to generate a detailed checklist. The chairpersons might ask each of their committee members to develop a list, then hold meetings to consolidate the lists into one master list. Each committee also should keep detailed records so others can repeat the bazaar next year.

The following ideas will help you begin thinking about the details you'll need to take care of.

Attracting dealers
Your bazaar will be only as good as the crafts that are sold. Therefore, the most important step is to attract top-quality dealers.

Compile a list of dealers whose work you have seen or who are recommended to you by friends. Also assign several people to go to crafts shows in your area and pick up cards from the dealers.

By July, the dealer chairperson should send out applications to dealers, asking that they return their applications and send color photographs of their crafts by September 1. Select the dealers you want from the applications, and send out official letters of invitation, along with guidelines for dealers.

As you choose the dealers, keep in mind that you'll need a variety of crafts. Include gift items, plus decorations, gift wraps, greeting cards, and novelty items. Survey local crafts stores to see what types of items are currently popular.

Entertaining Kids

Here are some activities to keep children busy and happy while their parents shop.
- Kids-only shopping. Set aside a special area at holiday bazaars so children can shop for gifts for their parents and friends. Price items appropriately to allowances.
- Dress-up. Let kids try on old party clothes, sports uniforms, and Halloween costumes. Include a mirror so they can admire their outfits.
- Coloring. Keep children amused for hours with paper and crayons or markers. Suggest a theme or two to spur their creativity.
- Face painting. Decorate kids' cheeks and foreheads with nontoxic water-soluble paints or theatrical makeup.

In your letter to the dealers, explain your fee for their booth space. You might want to set a standard space size, then charge a set fee for that space.

Though many dealers may bring their own tables (along with shelves and other display equipment), others may need to rent tables. If you can make this service available, charge a few dollars extra for each table you rent.

Publicizing the event
Make up preprinted postcards to send to all media that could give you free publicity. Include the time, place, and phone number of a contact person. By keeping the information brief and to the point, you'll make it easy for a radio announcer or editor to say what needs to be said about the bazaar.

Handling logistics
Before the bazaar, hold a "dry run" to make sure everything will work smoothly. Here are a few points to consider.
- You may need more than one entrance, especially if the weather is inclement, so that people won't have to stand outside. If you charge admission, stamp people's hands as they enter (using a festive stamp for fun) so they can come back later in the day if they like.
- Control the flow of the crowd, if necessary, by keeping track of the number of people entering, then letting a few out before admitting

more. This may be required by local fire regulations. Be sure to check beforehand.
● If the exhibit area is cramped, set aside an area where parents can park their strollers.
● Designate a smoking room, if need be, or put up no-smoking signs. In a crowded room, smoking can be dangerous, especially with small children around.

Feeding the crowds
Sales of refreshments can contribute handsomely to your fund-raising efforts. You might consider serving rolls and coffee in the morning, cookies and hot wassail throughout the bazaar, and possibly a simple lunch, too.

Be sure to provide a place for guests to sit and enjoy their refreshments. When your customers have a chance to rest this way, they'll get up refreshed and ready to continue shopping.

Bake sales, too, are naturals for bazaars. If volunteers can't bring baked goods, ask them to donate flour, chocolate chips, and other ingredients, then hold a big-batch baking party before the bazaar.

Decorating for better sales
Ask your dealers to make their booths look as attractive as possible. You might even offer a prize for the prettiest or most festive booth. This will improve the looks of the show as a whole and will help the dealers attract customers to their tables. ♠

December

—Elizabeth Coatsworth

Father loved surprises.

This year Christmas came on Friday, and Thursday morning he said to Cousin Mary and the children at breakfast, "We're leaving at ten. Get your suitcases packed for four days, and if you happen to have any pies or cake in the house you might bring them along. I'll pack a basket with supplies."

Four faces looked at him while four spoons hung forgotten in the air.

"Why, what do you mean?" asked Cousin Mary. "Ten o'clock tomorrow?"

"No, no, Cousin Mary. Father means ten o'clock today!" cried Jean, leaping from her chair to run around the table to hug her father. "It's today! Oh, where are we going?"

"Don't strangle me," said Father calmly, "and your porridge has to be eaten, you know, before you can go exploring. No, Lydia, there are no horses in this. And you'll all know where we are going when we get there."

Mark understood what was being said, but he was chiefly interested in one thing.

"Pie?" he repeated, like a little parrot. "Cake? I'll finish the pie."

"That's for the adventure, ducky," cried Jean gaily, finishing her porridge and banana much too fast. "Cousin Mary, may I please be excused? I have all the presents for the family to pack, too."

Cousin Mary protested a little more about so sudden a plan. She was accustomed to thinking about a plan until she was well used to it before she started to act on it. Even her new dresses were hung in her closet a month or two, until they seemed familiar, before she could bring herself to wear them. But since the children and now their father had come to live with her, she was really beginning to enjoy the excitement of doing things on the spur of the minute.

Still, when the children had thundered upstairs to make their beds and begin their packing, she said to their father, "Now that the children are gone, you can tell me where we are going."

But, no, he wouldn't tell. His eyes danced mischievously.

"It's to be a surprise for you all," he said. "You, most of all," and he began rummaging in the pantry and putting things like sugar and salt and flour in small tins and stowing them away in baskets to take with them.

By ten o'clock they were all ready. Everyone had begun by trying to bring too much; but in the end they had put most of the things back where they came from, and even then the luggage trunk at the back of the car, and the space at their feet, too, were pretty well filled. But no one minded that. At the last moment Cousin Mary remembered that she had forgotten about the hens, and jumped out of the front seat and hurried off to ask her next-door neighbor—who had hens of her own—if she would feed Cousin Mary's, too, for a few days.

Then they started off. They didn't turn down town but off to the highway past the old grain mill; beside the harbor, which looked gray under the gray sky; up old Colony Hill.

It was not a very cold day, and not a very pretty day, either. The sky was covered with clouds, and yet they didn't promise snow. Now and then the sun would glint through for a little and a silver gleam would appear on the gray water, and a pale glow strike across the withered grass and the leafless trees.

"It's not Christmas weather at all!" cried Lydia. "How can the Christ Child be born without a carpet of snow to spread about his stable, and a curtain of snow for the angels to fly through?"

continued

Jean did not imagine Christmas Eve that way.

"It was hot, Lydia," she said. "There were palm trees, and the camels stood about and the shepherds wore sandals without any stockings. There wasn't any snow. The star shone down through the hot warm night—like that time last July when we didn't even put our sheets over us. Isn't that true, Father?"

"Well," said Father, "neither was true. I had a friend who was in Jerusalem one Christmas and he said it was gray, with an icy wind and the dust blowing. There wasn't any snow, but he said he had never been colder in his life. There were camels on the hills, looking miserable, with their backs to the wind. And I guess the shepherds wore sandals, but they crouched behind the rocks and shivered over their little fires."

"*Our* Christmases," said Lydia with decision, "should be the way I've described. White and bright, and then the blue sky coming out; and every footprint should be new like the first footprint in the world, made by the first man . . . and the first mouse and the first rabbit and the first deer—"

"And the first everything," Jean summed up. "Father, where are we going?"

But Father only shook his head. They were going south, that much they could see.

"Plymouth?" coaxed Lydia, breathing down Father's neck. "Is it Plymouth?"

But Father shook his head.

"I won't tell."

Just before they came to the great bridge which crosses the Cape Cod Canal they got out for an early lunch, which only Mark and his father did justice to—the others were too excited to eat much. And then they drove on. Now they were on the cape, passing through pretty villages with white cottages and big elms and now and then seeing, across the distant dunes, the glint of the bay.

Still they drove on. At Orleans, Father got out to go into a grocery for final supplies.

As they waited in the car Jean said, "It's as though we were starting on a pirate cruise. Hush, Mark! Stop humming! I hear the waves breaking."

Now as they drove they caught glimpses of the sea—not the bay, as they had before, but the sea breaking in slow curlings of silver on miles of beaches, with dunes which they could see across the marshes.

Suddenly Father turned off on a side road and the car was heading straight out toward the ocean itself. They were on a bluff. The sea below them looked enormous. There were no headlands, no Milnot's light on its rocks, not even a ship. Only the sea gulls cried over the waves, and the little shore larks flew twittering over the harsh dune grass in the wind. There was a big white buillding behind them with a lookout on the roof.

"It's the Nauset Coast Guard Station. You'll see one of the men on the lookout now," said Father, but he drove on between the dunes and the marshes.

Unless one has driven on a dune road it would be hard to think of how it would twist and wind, now hard and smooth, now deep in the sand almost to the hubs of the car's wheels. In the bad places the road split into three or four roads. It wasn't easy to see which was the best, when all were bad. Cousin Mary held on tight and fixed her eyes far ahead. Yet, though they had to get out once or twice to push and put the boards under the tires, they arrived safely at the brown camp.

It was a shuttered building in the shelter of a high dune, with the grasses and lagoons of the marshes at its door and, far beyond, the pleasant uplands and the scattered white houses of Eastham. The roar of the waves shook the air. It was less cold here than in Hingham, but still it was gray with that waiting air.

"Here we are," said Father as they all sat rather breathlessly taking in their surroundings. "It belongs to Mr. Danvers at my office, and he suggested we might like to use it."

Father had taken from his pocket a Yale key fastened to a smooth little piece of driftwood.

"Just right," Jean thought.

He opened the door while the family waited in silence close behind him. It seemed dark and damp and musty inside, but Father hurried about opening the shutters. Jean, as eldest, was allowed to light the fire left all ready in the fireplace and, with that on the hearth and the light coming in the windows, the place began to look pleasanter. There was a big room with a fireplace at one end with chairs about it. Along one wall was a table with an oil lamp on it, and at the other end was a wood stove with scarlet saucepans hanging behind it on the brown wall. Cousin Mary began carrying blankets out from the bedrooms and spreading them on the beach-plum bushes to dry, and the children dragged in suitcases and groceries from the car.

Soon the place began to look as if it were theirs. Cousin Mary made hot chocolate, the little girls buttered rolls, and they sat down to a house-warming party.

But behind the dunes was the sea, endlessly bringing up its waves to tower like walls of glass and then hurl themselves down along the sands in long scallops edged with lace. Above the white scallops of the waves there ran a brown scallop of driftwood and seaweed, marking high

tide. After running races and skipping stones and mocking the sea gulls along the lonely beach, the family turned toward Nauset Station a mile away.

The sea was beautiful and wild and wonderful, but before very long all five were walking along the high-tide mark. It was very fascinating— the ocean's wastebasket, where it had spilled all the things it didn't want. There were pink crab shells, and grapefruit rinds and electric light bulbs (never broken) and bottles and kelp and sea gull feathers and mysterious bits of cloth, and painted markers for lobster pots and skeletons of fish. All at once Jean and Lydia gave a cry together and raced toward something which they saw ahead of them, lying like a great green fairy bubble among the seaweed. It was a ball of glass such as fishermen sometimes use for their nets or as buoys for their lobster-pots. It was the color of a wave, beautiful and unbroken.

Jean reached it first and scooped it up while Lydia watched her, panting.

"It's the most beautiful thing I ever saw," Lydia said bravely.

Jean came to a sudden decision.

"You may have it," she said.

Her gesture as she gave it to the astonished Lydia was a little grand, like a princess.

"Oh, Jean!" Lydia faltered.

The green glass ball was as close to magic as she had ever come.

"I don't want it," Jean said, beginning to skip away.

But the sea must appreciate generosity.

"What's that?" Cousin Mary asked suddenly. "Out there in the water?"

It was another glass ball, and a third one was already being played with in the froth along the beach. It took some time before the waves were

continued

willing to let the children have their treasures. They flung balls down at their feet and then hastily hauled them back down the shore and pounced noisily upon them again, only to throw them again to the children and then once more to change their minds. But in the end the sea gave them its present. Each child had a gift from the ocean, a little early for Christmas but not too early for their plans.

"That gives me an idea," Father said. "I'll borrow an ax at the station and cut down a little pine at the edge of the woods; and you children can trim it for a sea Christmas tree, with the three glass balls, first of all, and then anything else we can find along the beach—we've plenty of string."

The pink and lavender shells were, of course, pretty. The family chose only perfect ones. Then some of the seaweeds were nice, with colored stones held in their roots. They found several little bottles, too, which they filled with small pure-white pebbles kept shiny with sea water. Some one had the idea of fraying out an old rope to twist about the boughs like tinsel.

At the station several of the young men volunteered to come and help cut down the little pitch pine. As they walked up the sandy road they found bunches of gray bayberries to add to their skirtfuls, and cones from the larger of the little pitch pines which grew not far from the shore. Mark was beginning to tire, and a nice red-haired Coast Guardsman with freckles picked him up and carried him pick-a-pack. Another took a firm hold on the newly cut tree.

"We don't often have company on the beach at Christmas," they said. "We're off duty. You let us help."

As they passed the station the cook came running out with hot doughnuts in a bag.

"I'm no hand as a cook," he explained to Cousin Mary, "but perhaps these won't sink the ship."

And as he went back to his kitchen, they all called out, "Merry Christmas!"

The short way down the bluff to the beach was by a rough flight of stairs built along the face of the sand. For some reason the dunes here had shelved off and seemed to be made of black earth instead of sand. There were various black humps and bumps in the earth. Father spoke of them to the young men.

"They say that's peat. There used to be a cedar swamp here, a good many thousands of years ago, I've heard people say who study that kind of thing."

"It's at least twenty feet deep and with feet of sand on top of that, so the swamp must have been there a long time ago," Father said. "Would any of those logs burn?"

"Never thought of trying," the red-haired boy who was carrying Mark declared. "Why don't we dig one out?"

"A Christmas log that was a tree before the time of Christ," Jean murmured.

"A good deal before then," Father said.

He had laid down the basket and was helping to chop and pull and tug out a big log of wood. It was all black, almost as though it had turned to earth, but it had kept its shape. You could still see that it had once been a trunk with branches, too—something which had grown here when the shore had not been here at all, and when land creatures had roamed and hunted where the waves now broke.

They were tired that night and went to bed early, Cousin Mary and Jean and Lydia in the bunks in one room, Father and Mark in another.

Once Jean woke up and listened for a while to the splendid roar of the waves, but the next time she woke it was to hear Lydia's voice near the window.

"It's snowed! It's snowed! And Christ has been born into an ermine world!"

Jean ran to the window. Snow had come in the night, and the sun had followed it. The sky was bright, clear blue above the white dunes, and the sea gulls overhead were blindingly white. A smell of cooking came from the next room.

They rushed out, calling, "Merry Christmas! Merry Christmas, everyone!"

There hung their stockings lumpy and exciting looking; there stood the little pine tree covered with sea things and glass balls and shore berries like a mermaid's plaything, and the black log lay at the back of the freshly arranged fire.

"It's a Christmas log from the old days. If it burns we shall have good luck for a year. If it doesn't burn we shant," declared Jean. "May Lydia and I light it at the same moment? We must kneel down on the hearth and light it together."

"Me, too," said Mark, appearing tousled and half asleep in the door of his room.

Lydia smiled.

"Come here, ducky. I'll see that you don't burn your fingers."

While Father and Cousin Mary watched, the three children lighted the Christmas fire together and then sat back on their heels to look at it. Their lumpy Christmas stockings lay beside them, for a moment forgotten. The fire had caught the paper; its tongues shot up red among the driftwood. But the black Yule log—would that burn and bring them a happy year?

Now the flames were all about the ancient cedar, and yet it lay there as though made of iron. There was only the flapping sound of the fire, and the grumble of the sea on the beaches. And then it happened. The primeval log began to burn with a mane of small blue flames. The blue flames lengthened and turned yellow. The Yule log was burning. The year to come would be happy as this one had been.

"Merry Christmas!" they all called to one another again, turning to their presents—all but Mark, whose mouth was too full to say anything.

"You've eaten the candy cane from the top of the stocking!" accused Jean.

"You're a bad boy," Lydia said absent-mindedly, reaching for her stocking. Then she gave a groan. "You've eaten mine too!" she cried. "You're a very bad boy, Mark!"

"He's eaten mine, too," added Jean. "You're a very, very bad boy."

Mark licked his fingers in a business like way and began to dig into his little stocking like a terrier.

Christmas day had begun. Wonderful things were *always* beginning! ♣

Candies To Share

Here are some of the sweetest treats around! Perfect for a Christmas bazaar or for holiday gift giving, these homemade candies are sure to melt the heart of even the most inveterate Scrooge. For an extra-special touch, package the confections in gaily wrapped containers and add handmade greeting cards.

On the opposite page, clockwise, from top left, are *Raisin-Walnut Creams, Orange-Pecan Creams, Cherry-Almond Creams, Lollipops, Peanut Brittle, Cottage Brittle, Sour Cream Fudge,* and *Raisin-Pecan Clusters.* Recipes are on pages 34–37.

Sour Cream Fudge

1½ cups sugar
⅔ cup dairy sour cream
½ cup butter *or* margarine
8 ounces white
    confectioners' coating,
    finely chopped
1 teaspoon vanilla
¾ cup broken walnuts,
    toasted

Butter an 8x8x2-inch baking pan; set aside. Butter the sides of a heavy 2-quart saucepan. In saucepan combine sugar, sour cream, and butter or margarine. Cook over medium-high heat to boiling, stirring constantly with a wooden spoon. Clip a candy thermometer to side of pan.

Reduce the heat to medium. Continue cooking to 238° (soft-ball stage), stirring occasionally. Mixture should boil at a moderate, steady rate over entire surface. Remove from the heat.

Stir in confectioners' coating and vanilla, stirring till coating is melted. Add nuts; stir till smooth and creamy and mixture starts to thicken (about 3 minutes). Pour into the prepared pan. Score candy while warm into 1-inch pieces. Cool till firm. Cut into pieces. Store tightly covered. Makes 2 pounds (64 pieces).

Raisin-Cashew Clusters

1 cup raisins
1 pound roasted raw cashews
    or dry-roasted unsalted
    cashews
1 pound milk chocolate
    confectioners' coating

Place raisins in a steamer basket. Place over, but not touching, boiling water. Steam, covered, for 5 minutes. Let raisins stand at room temperature for 2 hours or till completely dry.

To roast raw cashews, spread in a shallow baking pan. Bake in a 350° oven for 15 minutes or till light brown.

In a large heavy saucepan melt confectioners' coating over low heat. Remove from heat. Stir in nuts. Add raisins; mix well. Drop by teaspoon onto a baking sheet lined with waxed paper. Let stand till firm. Store, tightly covered, in a cool place. Makes about 64.

Even the prettiest packaged sweet treats can be a disappointment if they're stale. So, keep mouth-watering morsels at their freshest by protecting them from air and moisture. Store them in a container with a tight-fitting lid or wrap them in plastic bags or plastic wrap before packaging them for a seasonal bazaar or for gift giving.

Royal Cream Fondant

If you want a batch of Raisin-Walnut Creams, Orange-Pecan Creams, and Cherry-Almond Creams, you'll need to make three separate batches of fondant. Never double or triple any candy recipe; you won't have successful results.

2½ cups sugar
½ cup milk
½ cup whipping cream
½ cup butter *or* margarine

Butter the sides of a heavy 3-quart saucepan. In the saucepan combine sugar, milk, cream, and butter or margarine. Cook over medium-high heat to boiling, stirring constantly with a wooden spoon. Clip a candy thermometer to side of pan. Reduce heat to medium and cook, stirring once or twice, till thermometer reaches 240° (soft-ball stage). Mixture should boil at a moderate, steady rate over entire surface.

Immediately pour into a 15x10x1-inch baking pan or onto a marble surface. *Do not scrape pan.* Cool, without stirring, about 25 minutes or just till slightly warm. Use a wooden spoon to scrape candy from edge to center, then beat vigorously for 4 to 8 minutes, till fondant is creamy and stiff. (Butter may seep out, but will blend in after beating.) Knead fondant with hands for 10 to 15 minutes or till free of lumps. Wrap in waxed paper or clear plastic wrap, then place in plastic storage bags. Refrigerate for at least 7 days or up to 1 month to ripen. Makes 1¼ pounds.

Raisin-Walnut Creams

1 recipe Royal Cream
   Fondant
½ cup chopped raisins
¼ cup brandy
½ cup chopped walnuts
1 pound dark chocolate
   confectioners' coating
   Finely chopped walnuts

Prepare Royal Cream Fondant and allow to ripen as directed. Combine raisins and brandy; cover and let stand for 24 hours. Drain well. Pat raisins dry on paper towels. Knead raisins and walnuts into ripened fondant. (If mixture is sticky, add sifted powdered sugar to fondant, 1 tablespoon at a time, and coat your hands with powdered sugar.) Shape candy into 1-inch balls. Place on a baking sheet lined with waxed paper. Let stand at room temperature, uncovered, for at least 1 hour or till a "crust" forms over surface of candy.

Dip candy in melted confectioners' coating (see Dipping Instructions, page 37). Place dipped candies on a baking sheet lined with waxed paper or a marble slab till dry and set. Sprinkle chopped nuts over tops of candy before chocolate coating is set. Makes about 1¾ pounds (70 pieces).

Orange-Pecan Creams

1 recipe Royal Cream
   Fondant
¼ teaspoon orange extract
3 drops yellow food coloring
   (optional)
2 drops red food coloring
   (optional)
½ cup finely chopped pecans
1 pound milk chocolate
   confectioners' coating

Prepare Royal Cream Fondant as directed, *except* after cooling make an indentation in fondant and add orange extract and food coloring, if desired. Continue beating and allow to ripen as directed.

Knead pecans into ripened fondant. Shape candy into 1-inch balls. Place on a baking sheet lined with waxed paper. Let stand at room temperature, uncovered, for at least 1 hour or till a "crust" forms over surface of candy.

Dip candy in melted confectioners' coating (see Dipping Instructions, page 37). Place dipped candies on a baking sheet lined with waxed paper or on a marble slab till dry and set. Makes about 1¾ pounds (70 pieces).

Cherry-Almond Creams

1 recipe Royal Cream
   Fondant
¼ teaspoon almond extract
4 drops cherry flavoring
   Few drops red food
   coloring (optional)
½ cup chopped almonds,
   toasted
¼ cup finely chopped candied
   red cherries
1 pound dark *or* milk
   chocolate confectioners'
   coating

Prepare Royal Cream Fondant as directed, *except* after cooling make an indentation in fondant and add almond extract, cherry flavoring, and food coloring, if desired. Continue beating and allow to ripen as directed.

Knead almonds and cherries into ripened fondant. (If mixture is sticky, add sifted powdered sugar to fondant, 1 tablespoon at a time, and coat your hands with powdered sugar.) Shape candy into 1-inch balls. Place on a baking sheet lined with waxed paper. Let candy stand at room temperature, uncovered, for at least 1 hour or till a "crust" forms over surface of candy.

Dip candy in melted confectioners' coating (see Dipping Instructions, page 37). Place dipped candies on a baking sheet lined with waxed paper or on a marble slab till dry and set. Makes about 1¾ pounds (70 pieces).

Peanut Brittle

2 cups sugar
1 cup light corn syrup
⅔ cup water
1 pound raw peanuts
1 tablespoon butter *or* margarine
1 teaspoon vanilla extract
2 teaspoons baking soda

Butter a 15x10x1-inch baking pan; set aside. Butter the sides of a heavy 3-quart saucepan. In saucepan combine sugar, corn syrup, water, and ½ teaspoon *salt*. Cook over medium-high heat to boiling, stirring constantly with a wooden spoon. Clip a candy thermometer to side of pan.

Cook over medium-low heat, stirring occasionally till the thermometer registers 240° (soft-ball stage). Stir in peanuts. Continue cooking over medium-low heat, stirring till thermometer registers 295° (hard-crack stage). Mixture should boil at a moderate, steady rate over entire surface. Remove from the heat; stir in butter or margarine and vanilla, stirring just till butter is melted. Immediately stir in baking soda. (Mixture will foam.) Pour candy into prepared pan. Do not spread candy. Cool completely. Store in a tightly covered container at room temperature. Makes 2¼ pounds.

Cottage Brittle

¾ cup broken pecans
¾ cup walnuts
¾ cup whole blanched almonds
¾ cup filberts
1½ cups sugar
1 cup light corn syrup
½ cup butter *or* margarine
1 teaspoon vanilla
1 teaspoon orange extract

Place all of the nuts in an 8x8x2-inch baking pan. Toast nuts in a 325° oven for 15 minutes, stirring twice. Butter a baking sheet; set aside. Butter a heavy 3-quart saucepan. In saucepan combine sugar, corn syrup, and butter or margarine. Cook over medium heat to boiling, stirring constantly with a wooden spoon. Clip a candy thermometer to side of pan.

Cook over medium heat, without stirring, till mixture reaches 290° (soft-crack stage). Mixture should boil at moderate, steady rate over the entire surface. Remove from the heat; remove thermometer. Stir in vanilla and orange extract. Stir in warm nuts. Immediately turn candy mixture out onto prepared baking sheet; spread evenly. Cool completely. Break brittle into pieces. Store in a tightly covered container at room temperature. Makes about 2¼ pounds candy.

Lollipops

2 cups sugar
⅔ cup light corn syrup
½ cup water
¼ teaspoon oil of cinnamon, cloves, peppermint, anise, *or* wintergreen
Few drops food coloring

If using lollipop molds, oil molds or spray with nonstick vegetable coating; attach the lollipop sticks. (Place sticks approximately halfway up the mold.)

Butter the sides of a heavy 2-quart saucepan. In saucepan combine sugar, corn syrup, and water. Cook over medium-high heat to boiling, stirring constantly with a wooden spoon. Cover with lid for 1 minute. Remove lid and reduce the heat to medium. Clip a candy thermometer to side of pan.

Continue cooking over medium heat, stirring occasionally, till the thermometer registers 300° (hard-crack stage). The mixture should boil at a moderate, steady rate over entire surface. Remove saucepan from the heat; remove thermometer. Stir in desired oil and food coloring. Immediately spoon mixture into molds. Let candy stand for 10 minutes or till firm. Invert molds; twist to remove candies. Cool completely. Store tightly covered. Makes 1¼ pounds.

Dipping Instructions

It's important that the creams stand at room temperature long enough to develop a "crust." This outer coating prevents the cream from dissolving when it's dipped into the warm coating. You can follow the package directions for melting confectioners' coating or use the directions that follow.

Break the confectioners' coating into a large heavy saucepan. Melt the coating over low heat, stirring constantly with a wooden spoon till smooth. Do not allow steam or water to drip into the coating. Remove coating from the heat. (Do not overheat or the coating will appear gray.)

Drop centers, one at a time, into the melted coating; turn to coat. Lift candy out of the coating with a long-tined fork, being careful not to pierce the candy center. Let excess coating drip off fork.

Draw the bottom of the fork across the rim of the pan to remove excess coating from it and the dipped candy. Invert the dipped candy onto a baking sheet lined with waxed paper. To swirl the coating on the top of the candy, twist the fork slightly as the candy falls. (If a large amount of chocolate coating pools at the base, next time allow more chocolate coating to drip off the fork before inverting the candy.)

Eggnog Fudge

A super-simple fudge, perfect for holiday gift giving. Be sure to attach a note that says to keep the fudge refrigerated.

  2 3-ounce packages cream
       cheese
  ½ cup dry instant eggnog
  ¼ teaspoon salt
4¾ cups sifted powdered sugar
  ½ cup chopped walnuts

Line an 8x8x2-inch baking pan with clear plastic wrap; set aside. Stir cheese to soften. Add dry eggnog and salt. Stir in powdered sugar. Add walnuts. Press mixture into the prepared pan. Chill till firm. Turn out. Cut fudge into 1½x1-inch pieces; wrap in clear plastic. Secure with tape or stickers. Refrigerate for up to 2 weeks. Makes 32 pieces.

No-Bake Fruitcake Balls

  1 5⅓-ounce can evaporated
       milk
  ¼ teaspoon shredded lemon
       peel
  3 tablespoons lemon juice
  2 tablespoons water
  3 cups graham cracker
       crumbs
1½ cups salted sunflower nuts
  1 cup diced candied cherries
  ¾ cup diced candied
       pineapple
  ¼ cup shredded coconut

In a small mixing bowl combine milk, lemon peel, lemon juice, and water. In a large mixing bowl combine graham cracker crumbs, sunflower nuts, candied fruits, and coconut.

Stir in milk mixture; mix well. Form into sixty 1-inch balls. Wrap in clear plastic wrap. Secure with tape or stickers. Store in the refrigerator. Makes 60.

A Treat for Santa

Youngsters are bursting with energy and excitement as Santa's arrival draws closer. To shorten the wait and channel all that exuberance, give them an afternoon in the kitchen, all in the name of jolly old Saint Nick.

Candy Cane Bread

2 cups all-purpose flour
¼ cup packed brown sugar
2 teaspoons baking powder
½ cup butter *or* margarine
¼ cup chopped peanuts
1 beaten egg
½ cup milk
  Powdered Sugar Icing
  Pressurized red and green decorater icing (optional)
  Red cinnamon candies (optional)

In a medium mixing bowl combine flour, brown sugar, baking powder, and ¼ teaspoon *salt.* Cut in butter or margarine till mixture resembles coarse crumbs. Add peanuts. Mix egg and milk; add to dry ingredients and stir till moistened.

On a lightly floured surface pat dough into 10x7-inch rectangle, ½ inch thick. Cut crosswise into 1-inch strips. Twist each strip; bend end around to form cane.

Place canes several inches apart on a greased baking sheet. Bake in a 425° oven for 10 minutes or till light brown. Carefully transfer to a wire rack; cool. Coat canes with Powdered Sugar Icing. Decorate with icing and candies, if desired. Makes 10.

Powdered Sugar Icing: Stir together 2 cups sifted *powdered sugar* and enough *milk* to make of drizzling consistency.

A Christmas Eve Thought

If Santa Claus should stumble,
   As he climbs the chimney tall
With all this ice upon it,
   I'm afraid he'd get a fall
And smash himself to pieces—
   To say nothing of the toys!
Dear me, what sorrow that would bring
   To all the girls and boys!
So I am going to write a note
   And pin it to the gate—
I'll write it large, so he can see,
   No matter if it's late—
And say, "Dear Santa Claus, don't try
   To climb the roof tonight,
But walk right in, the door's unlocked,
   The nursery's on the right!"

—Harriet Brewer Sterling

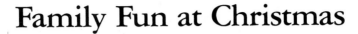

Family Fun at Christmas

Simply having the family together adds a special sparkle of joy to the Christmas holiday. But when you think back to past Christmas celebrations, what makes each year memorable is what you *did* together. It's the impromptu snowball fight, the gin rummy tournament that lasted till 2 a.m., the skit the little ones put on for the grown-ups, or the caroling at the old folks home that lingers in your hearts. These family fun times provide you with valuable resources for reminiscing with the family in years to come.

When planning family activities, let your family's personality, size, and mood determine what you do. Don't feel that every activity must be planned. Spur-of-the-moment fun is sometimes the most pleasurable. Likewise, don't schedule the family's time too strictly. After all, the holidays are a time for rest and relaxation. If the activity you suggest to the family is not received with unanimous enthusiasm, allow part of the family to do one thing while the rest does another. Sometimes regrouping around the dinner table to share experiences is as rewarding as doing one activity together.

Deck the House

Left to Mom and Dad, decorating the house for Christmas can be a dreaded task. Turn the job into a time of family togetherness and it's done in a fraction of the time with many times the pleasure.

Exterior decorating

Summon the troops to don the appropriate apparel and head outside for constructive and creative recreation. Voilà! An instant work crew to give the exterior of your house some special Christmas touches. To get the crew into the decorating mood, you might start with trimming a significant tree or hedge in your yard with outdoor lights and weatherproof accessories. Then delegate tall workers to hang door and window decorations. If you're lacking for such ornaments, send the family on a hunt for greenery and pinecones.

This may require transportation to a park where pine trees abound or even to a Christmas tree sale lot where branches can be picked up off the ground or bought for pennies. Use the smaller twigs for assembling wreaths. Tie a large bow on the larger boughs for mantel or door decorations. Collect the pinecones in a basket that will hang on the door. Spice up the basket by bundling some long cinnamon sticks with plaid ribbon and securing them to the top of the basket.

Luminarias

Nothing says "welcome to our home" more warmly than a driveway lined with luminarias, containers holding flickering candles. Start this project at Thanksgiving by reminding the family to save those empty plastic milk jugs. (You can also use lunch-size paper bags or special bags with cutout designs made for use as luminar-

ias.) Enlist someone to cut off the spouts of the milk jugs with heavy scissors or a knife. Fill the bottom of the jugs with sand to steady them and insert a candle in each. Space the containers on one or both sides of your driveway or the walk approaching the door. At sundown, gather the family outdoors for the lighting of the luminaries. Long matches make the lighting job easier and safer.

Tree trimming

For many families, one of the most cherished events of the weeks before Christmas is decorating the Christmas tree. If a fresh tree is your preference, the expedition to the Christmas tree lot for a cut tree or to a Christmas tree farm to cut your own promises great excitement, especially for youngsters. Once the tree is up, let the family have at it, starting with lights, then tinsel, then garlands, and lastly, the ornaments.

While you're decorating, don't forget the backyard trees. They are well-suited as Christmas trees for the birds. Have the kids string colorful strands of yarn or thread with popcorn, cranberries, marshmallows, or stale bread. Even little hands can make these ornaments by cutting shapes out of stale bread with cookie cutters, spreading them with peanut butter that has been tinted with red food coloring to attract the birds, and threading a brightly colored ribbon through the top for hanging.
continued

Frolic Outdoors

Suggest an outdoor recreational activity for the whole family and you're bound to get taken up on it. In climates where snow is the norm in winter, sledding, skating, tobogganing, downhill or cross-country skiing, snow mobiling, and snowsculpting are great ways to spend all or part of a day together. Delight the little ones by playing a rousing game of fox and geese or showing them how to make angels in the snow by lying on the ground, face up, and spreading arms and legs to make wings and a skirt.

For an extra-special experience, load the family into a hay wagon or sleigh pulled by a team of work horses at a local farm and delight your senses with the feel of the brisk air against your face and the sound of sleigh bells and laughter as you ride.

In warmer climates, picnics, hikes, or even family softball or football games in the backyard are great fun and great exercise.

Shop and Wrap

Make last-minute shopping a joy instead of a chore. Do it together. Pile into the car and descend on the downtown stores, the shopping mall, or a quaint shopping district. Undoubtedly, you'll need to divide up to conquer the task of buying one another gifts. At a set time, regroup and rejoice that your shopping is done!

Making your own Christmas wrapping paper can be an economical, enjoyable, and creative family effort. Buy inexpensive brown mailing paper or white butcher paper. Then search the house for any rubber stamps, stickers, felt-tip markers, crayons, and old magazines or Christmas cards for cutting out pictures or words. Let family members make their own designer wrapping paper, so the outsides of the gifts are as meaningful as the insides.

Soak In Sights And Sounds

Free time during the holidays allows you the perfect opportunity to check out local attractions. Museums, historic landmarks, planetariums, zoos, botanical gardens, and national monuments make good focal points for family outings. You may even learn something on your visit.

Revive Old Traditions

Many old-world Christmas customs have fallen by the wayside for one reason or another. Whatever your cultural heritage, it is certainly rich with tradition. Discover how your forefathers celebrated Christmas and revitalize these old practices. Many books, including this one, tell of ethnic holiday traditions that you can adopt in your own family. Some examples of these are hunting the Yule log, wassailing, stirring the Christmas pudding, and breaking a piñata. If your family's cultural background has a potpourri of origins, choose one tradition from each of the ethnic groups to bring to life again.

Share Quiet Times

Fireplace or no fireplace, gathering together in a cozy room at your house generates an inexpressable warmth among the family members. Check the program schedule for a TV Christmas classic that the family would enjoy. Or, rent a video movie for a night. The movies as well as the tape players rent for a modest price and provide a variety of viewing options for the family, from adventures to comedies to musicals. Put together a jigsaw puzzle— the bigger the better. Some friendly sibling rivalry in a card game or board game heats up the room even more.

Reading Christmas stories, poems, or plays aloud has been a practice in many households for generations, especially before the days of radio and TV. Whatever your literary interests, you'll find a wide array of holiday readings to choose from, with some excellent sources literally at your fingertips. (Turn to page 191 of this book for page numbers of stories and poems.) Once you have chosen a literary work to read, have one of the more outgoing family members start the narrative to draw the attention to the story. Involve the others by taking turns reading or assigning parts if it's a play.

Another quiet-time activity that more and more families are adopting as a tradition is the reading of Christmas cards when the family is together. All too often, the thoughtfulness of those who sent Christmas cards is not appreciated with the hubbub of activity during the holidays and the cards pile up in a basket till Christmas is over.

Set aside time (right after a meal is a good time) to have each person in the family read a card aloud so that everyone can think of the sender. Jog one another's memories with events that your family shared with these special people and relate up-to-date information about them.

For high-quality entertainment, treat the family to a Christmas play, ballet, or musical presentation put on by civic or religious groups.

Don Aprons

Cookie baking is one of those activities everyone shares in, even if participation means licking the bowl or taking in the aroma of freshly baked goodies. With a little encouragement, every family member can become part of the cookie factory assembly line. Assign the mixing, pan-greasing, cutting out or shaping, and decorating duties to your helpers. Be sure to switch jobs periodically to avoid a labor strike.

Building a gingerbread house or village is easier than it may seem. To make the construction flow smoothly, have the cookie pieces baked before you invite the construction workers to start
continued

their jobs. Set out frosting "mortar," some knives for spreading frosting, and an assortment of candy decorations to give distinction to the masterpiece. Your family's edible work of art makes a worthy centerpiece, as well as a conversation piece.

Celebrate Christmas Day

December 25 needs no activities to draw the family together. From waking to waning, it's a wondrous day of harmonious happenings. You can't hold onto that day, in the real sense, but you can do something to keep it within reach in your memory.

Gather the family in front of the tree and snap a photo. Frame it with festive fabric or a lightweight frame to hang on next year's tree.

For future reminiscing or for family members who were unable to be present, tape-record or videotape preparations for Christmas dinner, gift opening gaiety, or other family activities. Rerunning the tape shortly after the recording session promises great fun, too.

After Christmas

The days after Christmas can be disappointing after the emotional buildup to Christmas. Lessen the blow to your family with some creative fun.

Save some of your cookie baking until *after* Christmas. Gone is the hectic rush to get other things done. Now you can spend leisurely time shaping and decorating the cookies. The baking aroma will assure the family that December 26 was not the end of holiday fun.

The Scandinavians have a custom of celebrating the taking down of the Christmas tree. Referred to as plundering the tree, the event bestows merriment on an otherwise depressing task. The families involved in the celebration strip their respective trees and display the ornaments on a table, along with baked goods and other refreshments. The other families visit each of the houses, taking one ornament for use on their tree the following year. The barren trees are then gathered and burned while the families sing carols. Except for the burning of the trees, which may not be allowed in many American cities, this delightful tradition can easily be adapted to help lift sagging spirits in your home.

What will you do with those nice Christmas cards you received this year? They're too meaningful or pretty to throw away, but it's impractical to store them. Sit down with the family and several pairs of scissors for a gift-tag-making party. Use the scissors to cut out the prominent designs in the cards and, where possible, to cut through both the front and back of the cards to make folded tags. The final product will be lots of holiday tags for next year's packages. ♠

Winter Sports

It is the season meant for skates,
For ringing of the steel.
It is the season that we'll go
With merry toe and heel.
Across the lake and up the hill
We'll take a lively way.
All muffled to our neck and ears
Upon a winter day.
For Christmas fun is best when lived
Beneath the cold, blue sky,
And Christmas fun can mean the most
When snow drifts are piled high.
So skis to shoulder, off we go,
And knapsack on our back.
When flying down an icy hill
We'll never mind a pack.

We shout halloa across the vale!
We climb the highest peak.
Wherever danger seems to lurk,
That's just the spot we seek.
A hearty band on sled and skate,
You see us laughing by.
And you can't quench our mounting spirits
Hard though you may try!
For Christmas fun is best when lived
Beneath the cold, blue sky.
And Christmas fun can mean the most
When snow drifts are piled high.
So skis to shoulder, off we go,
And own the whole wide world!
Our red cheeks and our flying hair
A flag to skies unfurled!

Look at the Snow

Look at the snow!
Look at the snow!
Let's all take our sleds,
And go!
Up the hill we walk slow, slow,
And drag our red sleds in the snow;
But once at the top of the hill, we know
That like the wind they'll go, go, go,
Whizzing down to the flat, below.
Oh, the fun as we swiftly fly
Over the snow like a bird on high!
It takes our breath as our sleds speed by;
No one's as happy as you and I!
—Summers may come, and summers may go,
But we like the snow, the snow, the snow!

—*Mary Carolyn Davies*

Of Slopes and Sleds

Hurtling down the glistening white slope, eyes screwed shut against the prickly winter wind, and barely under control, you plummet toward the bottom of the hill. The fleeting magic is gone as you shakily get to your feet, brush off the powdery snow, grab the cord of your sled, and trudge back up the suddenly interminable slope.

For anyone who has grown up loving white winters, sledding is synonymous with the snow season. Sleds have come a long way from the earliest homemade versions: three boards nailed to two barrel staves, steered by leaning left or right and stopped by falling off or dragging a foot.

By the 1860s, most sleds on the slopes were factory-produced. A development

in 1889 led to the heydey of children's sled production a decade later, when more than 1,000 different models were on the market. That development was the introduction of the "Flexible Flyer," a sled that changed the face of the slopes forever. Invented by Sam Allen for his granddaughter, the revolutionary "Flexible Flyer" was many a kid's ultimate wintertime dream machine. It sported a steering suspension device in the front that permitted riders to plot their path by simply turning a wooden bar. For nearly 80 years it

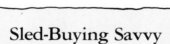

remained the only sled of its kind and is still popular today.

The late 1960s brought a proliferation of new sled designs with the introduction of high-density polyethylene, a cold-tolerant plastic. The modern material and designs produced an entirely new generation of lower-cost, lightweight sleds, some even fitted with steering wheels and brakes to make them safer.

With all the options available on sleds today, buying one has suddenly become much more complicated. But the simple truth is, whether your youngsters prefer the streamlined sleds popular today, or are intrigued with the daredevil sleds of your childhood, you can be sure that a good snow, a safe slope, and a sleek sled still spell winter fun for everyone. ♣

Sled-Buying Savvy

Consider these questions when a sled is on your shopping list:
● What type of snow do you most often have?

Wooden sleds with metal runners were designed for the packed snow of dirt roads and tracks. They perform best on hard-packed or crusty snows. Plastic models may be molded in one piece with wide, flat bottoms, or have wider, ski-like runners. This kind of sled is best in deep soft or slushy snow.

● What should you look for in a sled?

If you're buying a wooden sled, look for a platform of hardwood, treated with a weather-resistant coating. Check for cracks or splinters. Be sure the metal runners have no sharp edges and are securely fastened to the platform. Check plastic models for thin spots by holding them up against a light. Look for support ribs underneath or on the sides of

the sled for additional strength.
● Where will you find the best buys?

Once you decide what kind of sled you want, shop around for the best buy. Check major department stores, toy shops, sporting goods stores, hardware stores, or ski shops—and don't overlook the many mail-order possibilities as well. More than a dozen catalogs nationwide advertise a wide variety of sleds.

Christmas Wish List

For family gift ideas

What _____ wants for Christmas _____
_____
_____
_____

What _____ wants for Christmas _____
_____
_____
_____

What _____ wants for Christmas _____
_____
_____
_____

What _____ wants for Christmas _____
_____
_____
_____

What _____ wants for Christmas _____
_____
_____
_____

Holiday Crafts Projects

Crafts made as gifts or for bazaars

_____
_____
_____
_____
_____
_____
_____
_____
_____
_____
_____
_____
_____
_____
_____
_____
_____
_____
_____
_____
_____
_____
_____
_____
_____
_____
_____
_____
_____
_____

Holiday Foods

Foods made as gifts or for bazaars

_____
_____
_____
_____
_____
_____
_____
_____
_____
_____
_____
_____
_____
_____
_____
_____
_____
_____
_____
_____
_____
_____
_____
_____
_____
_____
_____
_____
_____
_____
_____

Letters to Santa

Dear Santa,

_____

_____

_____

_____

_____

_____

_____

_____

_____

_____

_____

_____

_____

_____

_____

_____

_____

_____

_____

_____

_____

_____

_____

From

Dear Santa,

_____

_____

_____

_____

_____

_____

_____

_____

_____

_____

_____

_____

_____

_____

_____

_____

_____

_____

_____

_____

_____

_____

_____

From

Seasonal Family Activities

Special outings and activities during the holidays
(see pages 40–45 for ideas)

Special Moments to Treasure

Photos and other holiday memorabilia

PRESERVING THE HERITAGE

Where Charity stands watching
And Faith holds wide the door,
The dark night wakes, the glory breaks,
And Christmas comes once more.

—from O Little Town of Bethlehem
by Phillips Brooks

Once on Christmas

—Dorothy Thompson

It is Christmas Eve—the festival that belongs to mothers and fathers and children, all over the so-called western world. It's not a time to talk about situations, or conditions, or reactions, or people who emerge briefly into the news. My seven-year-old son asked me this evening to tell him what Christmas was like when I was a little girl, before people came home for Christmas in airplanes, thirty odd years ago. And so I told him this:

A long, long time ago, when your mother was your age, and not nearly as tall as you, she lived with her mother, and father, and younger brother, and little sister, in a Methodist parsonage, in Hamburg, New York. It was a tall wooden house, with a narrow verandah on the side, edged with curley-cues of woodwork at the top, and it looked across a lawn at the church where father preached every Sunday morning and evening. In the backyard there were old Baldwin and Greening apple trees, and a wonderful, wonderful barn. But that is another story. The village now has turned into a suburb of the neighboring city of Buffalo, and fathers who work there go in and out every day on the trains and buses, but then it was just a little country town, supported by the surrounding farms.

Father preached in his main church there on Sunday mornings but in the afternoons he had to drive out to the neighboring village of Armor where there was just a little box of church in the middle of the farming country. For serving both parishes, he received his house and one thousand dollars a year. But he didn't always get the thousand dollars. Sometimes the crops were bad, and the farmers had no money, and when the farmers had no money the village people didn't have any either. Then the farmers would come to us with quarters of beef, or halves of pigs, or baskets of potatoes, and make what they call a donation. My mother hated the word, and

sometimes would protest, but my father would laugh, and say, "Let them pay in what they can! We are all in the same boat together."

For weeks before Christmas we were very, very busy. Mother was busy in the kitchen, cutting up citron and sorting out raisins and clarifying suet for the Christmas pudding—and shooing all of us out of the room, when we crept in to snatch a raisin, or a bit of kernel from the butternuts that my little brother was set to cracking on the woodshed floor, with an old-fashioned flat-iron.

I would lock myself into my little bedroom, to bend over a handkerchief that I was hemstitching for my mother. It is very hard to hemstitch when you are seven years old, and the thread would knot, and break, and then one would have to begin again, with a little rough place, where one had started over. I'm afraid the border of that handkerchief was just one succession of knots and starts.

The home-made presents were only a tiny part of the work. There was the Christmas tree! Mr. Heist, from my father's Armor parish, had brought it in from his farm, a magnificent hemlock, that touched the ceiling. We were transported with admiration, but what a tree to trim! For there was no money to buy miles of tinsel and boxes of colored glass balls.

But in the pantry was a huge stone jar of popcorn. When school was over, in the afternoons, we all gathered in the back parlor, which was the family sitting room. The front parlor was a cold place, where portraits of John Wesley and Frances Willard hung on the walls, and their eyes, I remember, would follow a naughty child accusingly around the room. The sofas in that room were of walnut, with roses and grapes carved on their backs, just where they'd stick into your back, if you fidgeted in them, and were

continued

covered with horsehair which was slippery when it was new, and tickly when it was old. But that room was given over to visits from the local tycoons who sometimes contributed to the church funds, and couples who came to be married.

The back parlor was quite, quite different. It had an ingrain carpet on the floor, with patterns of maple leaves, and white muslin curtains at the windows, and an assortment of chairs contributed by the Parsonage Committee. A Morris chair, I remember, and some rockers, and a fascinating cabinet which was a desk and a bookcase, and a chest of drawers, and a mirror, all in one.

In this room there was a round iron stove, a very jolly stove, a cozy stove that winked at you with its red isin-glass eyes. On top of this stove was a round iron plate; it was flat, and a wonderful place to pop corn. There was a great copper kettle, used for making maple syrup, and we shook the popper on the top of the stove—first I shook, until my arm was tired, and then Willard shook, until he was tired, and even the baby shook. The corn popped, and we poured it into the kettle and emptied the kettle, and poured it full again, until there was a whole barrelfull of popcorn, as white and fluffy as the snow that carpeted the lawn between the parsonage and the church.

Then we got a darning needle, a big one, and a ball of string. We strung the popcorn into long, long ropes, to hang upon the tree. But that was only half of it! There were stars to be cut out of kindergarten paper, red, and green, and silver, and gold, and walnuts to be wrapped in gold paper, or painted with gold paint out of the paintbox that I had been given for my birthday. One got the paint into one's fingernails, and it smelled like bananas. And red apples to be polished, because a shiny apple makes a brave show

on a tree. And when it was all finished, it was Christmas Eve.

For Christmas Eve we all wore our best clothes. Baby in a little challis dress as blue as her eyes, and I had a new pinafore of Swiss lawn that my Aunt Margaret had sent me from England. We waited, breathless, in the front parlor while the candles were lit.

Then my mother sat at the upright piano in a rose-red cashmere dress and played, and my father sang, in his lovely, pure, gay, tenor voice:

It came upon the midnight clear
That glorious song of old,
From angels bending near the earth
To touch their harps of gold.

And then we all marched in. It is true that we had decorated the tree ourselves, and knew intimately everything on it, but it shone in the dark room like an angel, and I could see the angels bending down, and it was so beautiful that one could hardly bear it. We all cried, "Merry Christmas!" and kissed each other.

There were bundles under the tree, most alluring bundles! But they didn't belong to Christmas Eve. They were for the morning. Before the morning came three little children would sit sleepily in the pews of their father's church and hear words drowsily, and shift impatiently, and want to go to sleep in order to wake up very, very, early!

And wake up early we did! The windows were still gray, and, oh, how cold the room was! The church janitor had come over at dawn to stoke the hot air furnace in the parsonage, but at its best it only heated the rooms directly above it, and the upstairs depended on grates in the floor, and the theory that heat rises. We shuddered out of our beds, trembling with cold and excitement, and into our clothes, which, when I was a little girl were very complicated affairs indeed. First, a long fleecelined union suit, and then a ferris waist dripping with buttons, then the cambric edged drawers edged with embroidery, and a flannel petticoat handsome with scallops, and another petticoat of cambric and embroidery, just for show, and over that a gay plaid dress, and a dainty pinafore. What polishing of cheeks, and what brushing of hair and then a grand tumble down into the warm, cozy back parlor.

Presents! There was my beloved Miss Jam-up with a brand new head! Miss Jam-up was once a sweet little doll, dears, who had become badly battered about the face in the course of too affectionate ministrations, and here she was again, with a new head altogether and new clothes, and eyes that open and shut. Scarfs and mittens from my mother's lively fingers. A doll house made from a wooden cracker box and odds and ends of wall paper, with furniture cut from stiff cardboard—and that was mother's work, too. And a new woolen dress, and new pinafores!

Under the tree there was a book: *The Water Babies,* by Charles Kingsley. To my beloved daughter Dorothy.

Books meant sheer magic. There were no automobiles—none for Methodist ministers, in those days. No moving pictures. No radio. But inside the covers of books was everything, everything that exists outside in the world today. Lovely, lovely words of poetry, that slipped like colored beads along a string; tales of rose-red cities, half as old as time. All that men can imagine, and construct, and make others imagine.

One couldn't read the book now. But there it lay, the promise of a perfect afternoon. Before one could get at it, one would go into the dining room. And what a dinner! This Christmas there was Turkey—with best wishes from one of my father's parishioners. And the pudding, steaming, and with two kinds of sauce. And no one to say, "No dear, I think one helping is enough."

We glutted ourselves, we distended ourselves, we ate ourselves into a coma, so that we all had to lie down and have a nap.

Then, lying before the stove, propped on my elbows, I opened the covers of my Christmas book.

"Once upon a time there was a little chimney sweep, and his name was Tom. He lived in a great town of the North Country . . . in England."

How well I knew that North Country, with its rows on rows of dark stone houses, its mine pits, its poor workmen. From such a town my father had come, across the ocean, to this village in up-state New York. I forgot Christmas, forgot everything, except the fate of little Tom. What a book! It wasn't just a story. There was poetry in it. The words of the poems sang in my head, so that after all these years I can remember them:

When all the world is young, lad,
And all the trees are green,
And every goose, a swan, lad,
And every lass a Queen;
Then hey for boot and spur, lad,
And 'round the world away;
Young blood must have its course, lad,
And every dog his day.

The little girl lay and dreamed that all the world was wide and beautiful, filled only with hearts as warm and hands as tender, and spirits as generous as the only ones she had ever known . . . when she was seven years old.

I wish you all a Merry Christmas! I wish us all a world as kind as a child can imagine it! ♣

Homespun Gifts and Toys

Richly textured gifts like these begin with inexpensive materials from your local discount store. Stitch a woven rug into a silly goose or stocking, turn tea towels into country cats, and transform a table runner into a horse or goat. The playful goose and rocking horse are less expensive still—they're crafted from fabric scraps you have on hand.

Rug Stocking And Duck

MATERIALS
Small rag rugs
¾ yard of 45-inch-wide denim
Thread
Butcher paper

INSTRUCTIONS
STOCKING: Enlarge the pattern, *right.*

Cut one stocking from the rug and one from denim. Cut a 6x18-inch denim band for the cuff.

With right sides facing, sew the front to the back, using ½-inch seams. Leave the top open. Sew over the seam three times to reinforce it. Clip the curves; turn to the right side.

Narrowly hem one long edge and both short ends of the cuff. With the right side of the cuff toward the wrong side of the stocking, fit the cuff inside the stocking, matching the raw edges and overlapping the short ends of the cuff at the stocking back.

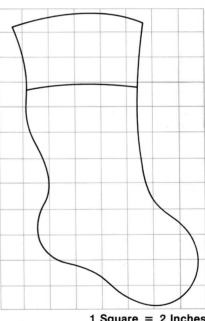

1 Square = 2 Inches

Sew ½ inch from the raw edges, securing the cuff to the stocking top with three rows of stitches. Turn the cuff right side out over the stocking and sew across the short ends of the cuff.

FOR THE DUCK: Enlarge the pattern, *below,* onto butcher paper and pin it to two layers of woven rug fabric.

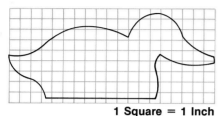

1 Square = 1 Inch

Machine-stitch through the paper and fabric along the outlines. Stitch over the lines three times. Leave openings for turning. Pull the paper away from the fabric. Trim the seams ¼ inch from the seam line. Turn right side out. Stuff and sew closed.

Country Cat

Shown on page 64.

MATERIALS
One 15x18-inch kitchen towel
Polyester fiberfill
Two ½-inch buttons
Black embroidery floss
Thread; butcher paper

INSTRUCTIONS
Enlarge the pattern, *right.* With right sides facing, fold the towel in half crosswise; pin the pattern to the towel. Machine-stitch ⅛ inch away from the pattern edge; leave the bottom open. Remove the pattern and trim the seam. Clip the curves; turn to the right side. Transfer eye, nose, and whisker markings to face of cat. Stuff and sew closed. Sew buttons for eyes at Xs marked on the pattern; embroider cat's nose and whiskers.

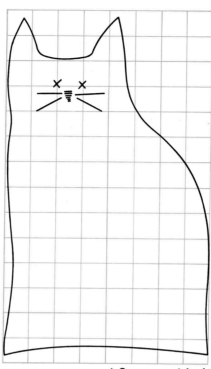

1 Square = 1 Inch

Rocking Horse

Shown on page 64.

MATERIALS
½ yard of 45-inch-wide red, pink, and purple patchwork fabric (or fabric scraps pieced into a patchwork pattern)
Small skein of purple hand-spun yarn
10x18-inch piece of ½-inch pine
Brads
Red fabric dye
White glue
Thread
Butcher paper
Polyester fiberfill

INSTRUCTIONS
Enlarge the pattern, *right.*
For the rockers, use a jigsaw to cut two arcs from pine. Also cut two 1¼x2-inch rectangles for

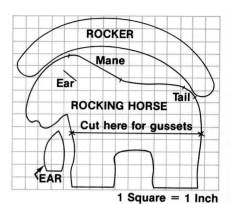

1 Square = 1 Inch

spacers. Nail the spacers between the rockers (horizontally) about 4 inches from the ends.

To dye the rockers, mix the fabric dye in an enameled kettle or sink, following the manufacturer's instructions. Float the rockers in the dyebath, turning them over every minute or so until you achieve the desired shade.

Remove the rockers from the dyebath, blotting the drips on a rag. Stand them on a waxed-paper surface to dry. Clean the sink, kettle, or other surface with household cleanser.

For the horse, cut the yarn mane (sixty-five 6-inch lengths) and tail (twenty 8-inch lengths). Adding ½-inch seam allowances, cut one horse and two ears from a double layer of patchwork fabric; cut a gusset, following the markings on the pattern.

Sew the mane and tail in place on the right side of one horse, fastening the ends securely ½ inch from the raw edge. With right sides facing, sew the upper halves of the horse together between the Xs, using ½-inch seam allowances. Turn the horse right side out.

Pin the right sides of the gusset (inside leg) pieces to the right sides of the horse. Sew the leg sides of the horse. Sew the leg seams (around the legs to the Xs), leaving the long edge of the gusset open. Clip the curves; turn the legs right side out. Stuff the horse firmly and stitch closed.

Secure the horse to the rockers with thread; slide glue between the fabric and wood. When the glue is dry, remove the threads.

Goat

Shown on page 64.

MATERIALS

Handwoven napkins, place mats, or table runner
Polyester fiberfill
Thread
Butcher paper

INSTRUCTIONS

Enlarge the pattern, *below,* onto butcher paper and pin it to two layers of woven fabric.

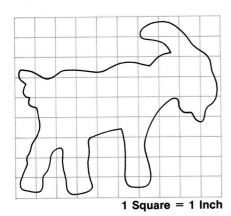

1 Square = 1 Inch

Machine-stitch through the paper and fabric along the outlines. Stitch over the lines three times. Leave openings for turning. Pull paper away from the fabric. Trim the seams ¼ inch from the seam line. Turn right side out. Stuff and sew closed.

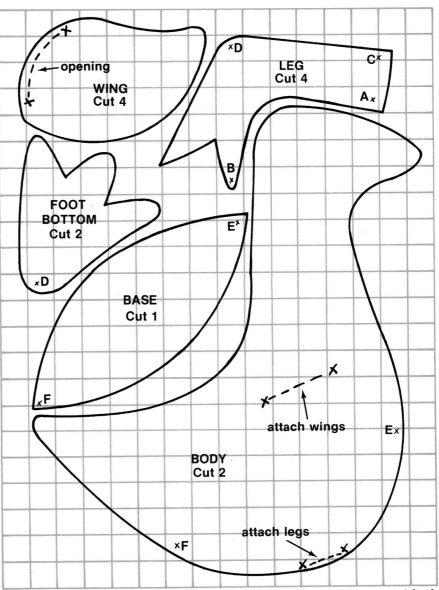

1 Square = 1 Inch

Goose

Shown on page 64.

MATERIALS

¾ yard of 45-inch-wide patchwork fabric (or scraps of fabric pieced into a patchwork pattern)
Polyester fiberfill
Thread
Butcher paper

INSTRUCTIONS

Enlarge the pattern, *above.*

With right sides facing, and using ½-inch seam allowances, sew the wings together; leave open between Xs. Turn right side out; press. Slip-stitch the wings closed and attach them to the body on each side between the Xs.

For legs, stitch the front seam on each leg (A to B). Sew the legs to the bottoms of the feet, ending at D. Sew back seams (C to D). Turn right side out and stuff. Attach to main body between Xs.

With right sides facing, sew the body together; leave open between E and F. Stitch the underside between points E and F (with the legs tucked inside), leaving an opening for turning. Turn right side out; stuff and stitch closed.

Festive Poinsettia Quilt

Stitch the traditions of Christmas into an heirloom-quality quilt you'll treasure for many Christmases to come.

Finished size is 82x91 inches.

MATERIALS
10 yards of unbleached muslin (5 yards for quilt top; 5 yards for backing)
2 yards of red cotton
Scraps of green and yellow cotton
82x91 inches of quilt batting
Blue pearl cotton embroidery thread
Off-white quilting thread
Graph paper
Sandpaper or cardboard for templates
Quilting frame or hoop
Red bias strips or bias tape
Water-erasable pen

INSTRUCTIONS
The quilt has a total of nine poinsettia designs—one in each corner, one centered along each side, and one in the middle. Each poinsettia is different, but all are adapted from the same basic pattern, page 70.

continued

To make a quilt exactly like the one pictured, refer to the photograph for the adaptations of the poinsettia pattern. But if you wish, you can alter the pattern, adjusting the size and shape of the poinsettias to fit your quilt.

For instance, you can appliqué two poinsettias in one flowerpot, or show them without the flowerpot. Whatever you decide, sketch the quilt you intend to make before you start to be sure you're satisfied with the overall design.

Before cutting the appliqués, preshrink all the fabric. Enlarge the pattern, *right.* Number the individual shapes in the appliqué design and note how many of each shape you'll need to cut.

To make the templates, trace each pattern piece onto sandpaper or cardboard. Do not add seam allowances. Because the flower petals are not all the same shape, make a template for each. When you have traced all the pieces, carefully cut out the templates.

With a water-erasable pen, lightly draw around each template on the fabric, leaving at least ½ inch between the pieces to allow for ¼-inch seam allowances all around. Trace around the templates for all appliqué pieces before you begin to cut.

When cutting out the fabric shapes, cut ¼ inch beyond the marked lines. After cutting the ap-

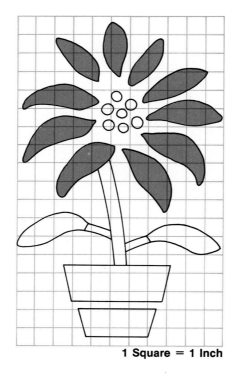

1 Square = 1 Inch

pliqués, sort them according to shape and color. Turn under seam allowances on the appliqués, then baste and press.

Cut and piece the muslin top to 72x81 inches. Lay the muslin out flat and arrange the appliqués in place. When you are pleased with the arrangement, pin and baste the appliqués to the muslin; whipstitch them into place.

Where the stem, flowerpot, and petals overlap more than ¼ inch, trim the excess fabric from the bottom shape to reduce bulk and eliminate shadows.

When you have appliquéd all of the pieces, make a border for the quilt as follows: Cut and piece 5½-

inch-wide strips of red fabric to equal the length of the quilt sides. Then, using a ¼-inch seam allowance, stitch the two strips to each side of the quilt top. Following the same procedure, cut, piece, and stitch borders for the ends of the quilt.

To prepare for quilting, cut and piece a muslin backing to match the quilt top. Layer the backing, batting, and quilt top. If you don't plan to use a full-size frame for quilting, baste the layers together from the center toward the sides and corners and around the edges.

Stretch the quilt in a frame or hoop. Quilt around each appliqué, then stitch the background in the pattern of your choice. We used blue pearl cotton to work five-pointed stars (each approximately 10 inches in diameter), and 4-inch-diameter circles stitched at random between the stars and the appliqués.

For a star pattern, make a template of a star from cardboard or sandpaper. Using a water-erasable pen, lightly trace around the template wherever you want the stars to appear on the quilt. Quilt over the outlines, using small running stitches. Finish the outside edges of the quilt with red bias strips or bias tape.

Painted Rocking Horse

Delight a youngster Christmas morning with an heirloom rocking horse you built yourself. It's made from pine, using basic tools, then finished with folk-art-style flourishes.

MATERIALS
1x8x9-inch piece of pine
14-inch length of 2x4 pine
2x4-foot piece of ½-inch-thick particleboard
¾x6¾-inch dowel
Finishing nails; 2¼-inch screws
Wood glue; putty
Red enamel; acrylic paints
Brushes
Graphite paper
Pecan ink; varnish

INSTRUCTIONS
Enlarge the patterns, *right.* The body of the horse is a shaped 2x4, clad on the top and sides with particleboard. Cut the 2x4 according to the seat top and end view patterns. Cant the sides at 13 degrees; cant in the ends ½ inch from bottom to top.

Cut the particleboard seat top according to the pattern. From one end, cut a ¾-inch-wide notch 4⅝ inches long to accept the head. Glue and nail the top onto the 2x4. Cant the edges flush. Cut the head from 1x8-inch pine; position it in the seat notch. Drill holes up through the 2x4 into the head; set the head aside.

Cut two particleboard sides to shape; round the edges with a

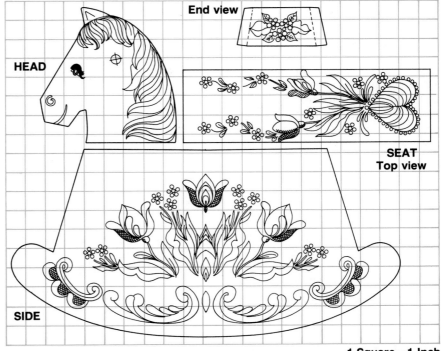

HEAD

End view

SEAT
Top view

SIDE

1 Square = 1 Inch

router. Glue and nail the rockers to the sides of the seat. Sand the edges smooth. Drill a hole in the head for the dowel as indicated on the pattern. Glue the head into the notch; secure with screws. Insert dowel; glue.

Sand the horse smooth and paint it red. Let dry, then sand and repaint it. Transfer the designs with graphite paper. Paint the rocker edges; fill in the shapes with desired colors. Double-load the paintbrush for shading; add details with a fine brush. Antique the horse with pecan ink. Let the finish dry; varnish.

Safe-and-Simple Woodburned Crèche

Your holiday handiwork will earn a place of honor when you make this easy Christmas crèche. Once Mom or Dad cuts out the shapes and drills the holes, you can use a woodburning tool to "draw" the designs on the wood. Be sure to practice on scraps first.

MATERIALS

¾x12x36 inches of pine
Scraps of ½-inch pine
⅛x6-inch dowel
Scrap of fake lamb's wool
Woodburning tool
Graphite paper; glue

INSTRUCTIONS

First, trace the patterns, *below,* onto a sheet of plain paper. Using graphite paper, transfer the patterns onto the wood. Transfer the arch above the cradle and the scythe blade onto ½-inch pine, and the rest to the ¾-inch pine.

Ask Mom or Dad to cut out the pieces with a jigsaw. Also cut a free-form five-pointed star from ¾-inch pine. Sand the edges of the pieces smooth. To use the woodburning tool, follow all the instructions that came with it. Be careful not to press too hard or to leave the tool in one spot for too long. Use it like a pencil, "drawing" the designs onto the wood. Follow all the design lines that

you transferred. On the star, wood-burn an outline about ¼ inch inside the edge.

Cut a scrap of fake fur for the lamb's body; glue it to the wood. Glue the arch over the infant's cradle. Ask Mom or Dad to drill a hole through the peasant man's hand and into the underside of the scythe blade to hold the handle (a ⅛-inch dowel). Glue the dowel into the blade, then slip it through the hole in the hand and glue it into place.

1 Square = 1 Inch

The Gift of the Magi

—O. Henry

One dollar and eighty-seven cents. That was all. And sixty cents of it was in pennies. Pennies saved one and two at a time by bulldozing the grocer and the vegetable man and the butcher until one's cheeks burned with the silent imputation of parsimony that such close dealing implied. Three times Della counted it. One dollar and eighty-seven cents. And the next day would be Christmas.

There was clearly nothing to do but flop down on the shabby little couch and howl. So Della did it. Which instigates the moral reflection that life is made up of sobs, sniffles, and smiles, with sniffles predominating.

While the mistress of the home is gradually subsiding from the first stage to the second, take a look at the home. A furnished flat at $8 per week. It did not exactly beggar description, but it certainly had that word on the lookout for the mendicancy squad.

In the vestibule below was a letter-box into which no letter would go, and an electric button from which no mortal finger could coax a ring. Also appertaining thereunto was a card bearing the name "Mr. James Dillingham Young."

The "Dillingham" had been flung to the breeze during a former period of prosperity when its possessor was being paid $30 per week. Now, when the income was shrunk to $20, the letters of "Dillingham" looked blurred, as though they were thinking seriously of contracting to a modest and unassuming D. But whenever Mr. James Dillingham Young came home and reached his flat above he was called "Jim" and greatly hugged by Mrs. James Dillingham Young, already introduced to you as Della. Which is all very good.

Della finished her cry and attended to her cheeks with the powder rag. She stood by the window and looked out dully at a gray cat walking a gray fence in a gray backyard. Tomorrow would be Christmas Day, and she had only $1.87 with which to buy Jim a present. She had been saving every penny she could for months, with this result. Twenty dollars a week doesn't go far. Expenses had been greater than she had calculated. They always are. Only $1.87 to buy a present for Jim. Her Jim. Many a happy hour she had spent planning for something nice for him. Something fine and rare and sterling—something just a little bit near to being worthy of the honor of being owned by Jim.

There was pier-glass between the windows of the room. Perhaps you have seen a pier-glass in an $8 flat. A very thin and very agile person may, by observing his reflection in a rapid sequence of longitudinal strips, obtain a fairly accurate conception of his looks. Della, being slender, had mastered the art.

Suddenly she whirled from the window and stood before the glass. Her eyes were shining brilliantly, but her face had lost its color within twenty seconds. Rapidly she pulled down her hair and let it fall to its full length.

Now, there were two possessions of the James Dillingham Youngs in which they both took a mighty pride. One was Jim's gold watch that had been his father's and his grandfather's. The other was Della's hair. Had the Queen of Sheba lived in the flat across the airshaft, Della would have let her hair hang out the window some day to dry just to depreciate Her Majesty's jewels and gifts. Had King Solomon been the janitor, with all his treasures piled up in the basement, Jim would have pulled out his watch every time he passed, just to see him pluck at his beard from envy.

So now Della's beautiful hair fell about her rippling and shining like a cascade of brown waters. It reached below her knee and made itself almost a garment for her. And then she did it up again nervously and quickly. Once she faltered for a minute and stood still while a tear or two splashed on the worn red carpet.

On went her old brown jacket; on went her old brown hat. With a whirl of skirts and with the brilliant sparkle still in her eyes, she fluttered out the door and down the stairs to the street.

Where she stopped the sign read: "Mme. Sofronie. Hair Goods of All Kinds." One flight up Della ran, and collected herself, panting. Madame, large, too white, chilly, hardly looked the "Sofronie."

"Will you buy my hair?" asked Della.

"I buy hair," said Madame. "Take yer hat off and let's have a sight at the looks of it."

Down rippled the brown cascade.

"Twenty dollars," said Madame, lifting the mass with a practised hand.

"Give it to me quick," said Della.

Oh, and the next two hours tripped by on rosy wings. Forget the hashed metaphor. She was ransacking the stores for Jim's present.

She found it at last. It surely had been made for Jim and no one else. There was no other like it in any of the stores, and she had turned all of them inside out. It was a platinum fob chain simple and chaste in design, properly proclaiming its value by substance alone and not by meretricious ornamentation—as all good things should do. It was even worthy of The Watch. As soon as she saw it she knew that it must be Jim's. It was like him. Quietness and value—the description applied to both. Twenty-one dollars they took from her for it, and she hurried home with the 87 cents. With that chain on his watch Jim might be properly anxious about the time in any company. Grand as the watch was, he sometimes looked at it on the sly on account of the old leather strap that he used in place of a chain.

When Della reached home her intoxication gave way a little to prudence and reason. She got out her curling irons and lighted the gas and went to work repairing the ravages made by generosity added to love. Which is always a tremendous task, dear friends—a mammoth task.

Within forty minutes her head was covered with tiny close-lying curls that made her look wonderfully like a truant schoolboy. She looked at her reflection in the mirror long, carefully, and critically.

"If Jim doesn't kill me," she said to herself, "before he takes a second look at me, he'll say I look like a Coney Island chorus girl. But what could I do—oh! what I could do with a dollar and eighty-seven cents?"

At 7 o'clock the coffee was made and the frying-pan was on the back of the stove hot and ready to cook the chops.

continued

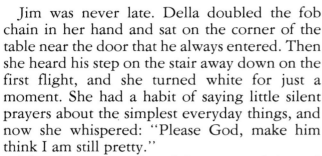

Jim was never late. Della doubled the fob chain in her hand and sat on the corner of the table near the door that he always entered. Then she heard his step on the stair away down on the first flight, and she turned white for just a moment. She had a habit of saying little silent prayers about the simplest everyday things, and now she whispered: "Please God, make him think I am still pretty."

The door opened and Jim stepped in and closed it. He looked thin and very serious. Poor fellow, he was only twenty-two—and to be burdened with a family! He needed a new overcoat and he was without gloves.

Jim stopped inside the door, as immovable as a setter at the scent of quail. His eyes were fixed upon Della, and there was an expression in them that she could not read, and it terrified her. It was not anger, nor surprise, nor disapproval, nor horror, nor any of the sentiments that she had been prepared for. He simply stared at her fixedly with that peculiar expression on his face.

Della wriggled off the table and went for him.

"Jim, darling," she cried, "don't look at me that way. I had my hair cut off and sold it because I couldn't have lived through Christmas without giving you a present. It'll grow out again—you won't mind, will you? I just had to do it. My hair grows awfully fast. Say 'Merry Christmas!' Jim, and let's be happy. You don't know what a nice—what a beautiful, nice gift I've got for you."

"You've cut off your hair?" asked Jim, laboriously, as if he had not arrived at that patent fact yet even after the hardest mental labor.

"Cut it off and sold it," said Della. "Don't you like me just as well, anyhow? I'm me without my hair, ain't I?"

Jim looked about the room curiously.

"You say your hair is gone?" he said, with an air almost of idiocy.

"You needn't look for it," said Della. "It's sold, I tell you—sold and gone, too. It's Christmas Eve, boy. Be good to me, for it went for

you. Maybe the hairs of my head were numbered," she went on with a sudden serious sweetness, "but nobody could ever count my love for you. Shall I put the chops on, Jim?"

Out of his trance Jim seemed quickly to wake. He enfolded his Della. For ten seconds let us regard with discreet scrutiny some inconsequential object in the other direction. Eight dollars a week or a million a year—what is the difference? A mathematician or a wit would give you the wrong answer. The magi brought valuable gifts, but that was not among them. This dark assertion will be illuminated later on.

Jim drew a package from his overcoat pocket and threw it upon the table.

"Don't make any mistake, Dell," he said, "about me. I don't think there's anything in the way of a haircut or a shave or a shampoo that could make me like my girl any less. But if you'll unwrap that package you may see why you had me going a while at first."

White fingers and nimble tore at the string and paper. And then an ecstatic scream of joy; and then, alas! a quick feminine change to hysterical tears and wails, necessitating the immediate employment of all the comforting powers of the lord of the flat.

For there lay The Combs—the set of combs, side and back, that Della had worshipped for long in a Broadway window. Beautiful combs, pure tortoise shell, with jewelled rims—just the shade to wear in the beautiful vanished hair. They were expensive combs, she knew, and her heart had simply craved and yearned over them without the least hope of possession. And now, they were hers, but the tresses that should have adorned the coveted adornments were gone.

But she hugged them to her bosom, and at length she was able to look up with dim eyes and a smile and say: "My hair grows so fast, Jim!"

And then Della leaped up like a little singed cat and cried, "Oh, oh!"

Jim had not yet seen his beautiful present. She held it out to him eagerly upon her open palm. The dull precious metal seemed to flash with a reflection of her bright and ardent spirit.

"Isn't it a dandy, Jim? I hunted all over town to find it. You'll have to look at the time a hundred times a day now. Give me your watch. I want to see how it looks on it."

Instead of obeying, Jim tumbled down on the couch and put his hands under the back of his head and smiled.

"Dell," said he, "let's put our Christmas presents away and keep 'em a while. They're too nice to use just at present. I sold the watch to get the money to buy your combs. And now suppose you put the chops on."

The magi, as you know, were wise men—wonderfully wise men—who brought gifts to the Babe in the manger. They invented the art of giving Christmas presents. Being wise, their gifts were no doubt wise ones, possibly bearing the privilege of exchange in case of duplication. And here I have lamely related to you the uneventful chronicle of two foolish children in a flat who most unwisely sacrificed for each other the greatest treasures of their house. But in a last word to the wise of these days let it be said that of all who give gifts these two were the wisest. Of all who give and receive gifts, such as they are wisest. Everywhere they are wisest. They are the magi. ♠

77

Christmas Symbols

At Christmastime, even the simplest things take on an almost magical quality. Whether it's a compliment from a loved one, a blossoming plant, or a card from a faraway friend, it's the stuff of which memories are made. These are just a few of the symbols we use at Christmas to help us celebrate the season and how they came to be.

Christmas trees

Since days long ago, people have invited the spirit of the woods into their homes and enjoyed the brilliant greens of the pines, the firs, and the spruces. But it was St. Boniface, a German, who is credited with the first Christmas tree. It is said that when he cut down a sacred oak tree to illustrate the end of old pagan beliefs, a fir tree sprang up in its place. St. Boniface declared the tree holy and said its evergeen boughs were a sign of immortality and pointed toward heaven.

Not until the early 17th century, did the Christmas tree really take root as a part of the Christmas celebration. From Europe, the tradition crossed the English Channel with Prince Albert (Queen Victoria's German husband) in 1841 and on to America with German immigrants.

The custom of stringing lights on trees in public areas or on front lawns was developed by those who saw the practice as being symbolic of Christ, "the Tree of Life," who freely gives His sacred gifts of light, life, and wisdom to all people.

Candles

Although no candle was lighted in the stable at Bethlehem, it nevertheless has become a universal yuletide decoration.

Christians use candles to represent Christ as the "Light of the World." Candle wax symbolizes His body; the candlewick, His soul; and the flame, His divinity for all to see. Many churches in America today celebrate Christmas Eve with candlelight services in which the soft light represents the enlightenment that Christ brought to the world.

At Christmases past, people placed candles in their windows to light the way for weary travelers. It was thought the Christ Child would come to their homes in the form of a stranger, to see if they would welcome Him openly.

Candles burned at Christmas also were believed to have magical powers and, therefore, were never simply thrown away. Farmers might feed the candle stubs to chickens, mark cattle with the sign of the cross, or rub candle wax on their plows to bring good luck and good crops in the coming year.

CHRISTMAS

Santa Claus

Santa Claus hasn't always been the jolly, jelly-bellied chap we know and love today. He is actually a version of "St. Nicholas," believed to have been a 4th-century Turkish archbishop devoted to charity. A popular story about St. Nicholas establishes the custom of hanging stockings by the chimney. When he learned of a nobleman who had no money to marry off his daughters, St. Nicholas tossed three bags of gold into the nobleman's house as he rode by. One bag fell into a stocking that had been hung by the fireplace to dry. The legend soon spread throughout Europe and then made its way to America with Dutch immigrants, who called St. Nicholas *Sinterklaas.*

Clement Clarke Moore was the first American to describe Santa, in his 1822 poem "A Visit from St. Nicholas," also known as "The Night Before Christmas." Some 40 years later, Thomas Nast, the political cartoonist who designed our Republican elephant and Democratic donkey symbols, used Moore's description of Santa for a drawing published in *Harper's Weekly.* Before that time, St. Nick had been depicted as anything from a tiny woodland troll to a stern religious figure in robes of various colors. Nast even created the red suit, a remnant from a Civil War cartoon that portrayed Santa wearing a red, white, and blue suit in support of the Union. In addition to bringing Santa's image to life, Nast also brought Santa's actions to life, including his keeping records of good and bad children, and having a workshop full of toys and elves.

By any name, be it *Père Noel* in France, Father Christmas in England, *Kris Kringle* in Germany, or Grandfather Frost in Russia, this jolly bearer of gifts and good cheer is loved by one and all.

Carols

It was natural that the telling of Christmas tales should move into music. First came the religious hymns, and then the carols as we know them today, which treat religious topics in a more familiar and festive way.

Because Christmas is the only celebration for which carols were specifically written, the word "carol" is now interpreted as simply a Christmas song.

St. Francis of Assisi is considered the "father of the carol," and Italy, its birthplace. From Italy, the carol emigrated to Spain, France, Germany, and eventually throughout the world, but it never lost its endearing trait of being in the common language for the common people.

Crèches

In Provence, an area in southern France, the popularity of nativity scenes in churches spread to families, who began setting up their own crèches at home. Created in 1223 by an Italian friar who came to be known as St. Francis of Assisi, the crèche has become a beloved Christmas symbol. Children and adults alike never tire of hearing the story of the Baby Jesus.

Inspired by his visit to Bethlehem, St. Francis wished to share his moving experience with others. So, he engaged local craftsmen to build the first crèche in a nearby cave. On Christmas Eve, he once again told the story of Christ's birth, and to the people assembled there, it was as if they, too, had been in Bethlehem and had witnessed the miracle of Christmas.

Christmas Symbols

Christmas is indeed a time of celebration. It's a time to celebrate love—the love of family and friends, and the love of God for us all. It's a time to celebrate hope—the hope that shone so brightly in the sky over Bethlehem and continues to light our lives throughout the year. And it's a time to celebrate peace—peace and goodwill to all people for all time.

Wassail

"Wassail!" or "To your good health!" is an old Anglo-Saxon drinking pledge, and should be answered with "Drinkhaile!" Served from a very large bowl at Christmas, Twelfth Night, and New Year's Eve, wassail is a hot punch also known as lamb's wool. It's made of ale, sugar, spices, eggs, and baked apples. The good cheer and luck thought to come from drinking wassail to the health of one another was carried door to door.

Boxing day

December 26, St. Stephen's birthday, also is known as "Boxing Day" and was at one time nearly as important as Christmas Day. On this day, the village priest would distribute the contents of the church's alms boxes to the poor people of the village. Now, Christmas "boxes" are given to servants and public service people such as newspaper and mail carriers, garbage collectors, and police officers. The "box," or money, usually is given the week before Christmas, but originally those who expected to be tipped appeared on Boxing Day.

Bells

Many years ago in Dewsbury, England, a great bell would toll on Christmas Eve for the entire hour before midnight. "Tolling the Devil's knell," it was said, gave the Devil notice of Christ's approaching birth. For it was at the Saviour's birth, that the Devil died.

Yuletide bells have inspired poets and songwriters in many countries to put their imagery to verse. Longfellow's message of peace in "I hear the bells on Christmas Day" remains a favorite, as does Charles Wesley's "Hark! The Herald Angels Sing," believed written after the author heard chimes one Christmas morning.

Whatever we may think when we hear holiday chimes, we can appreciate the beautiful music and message of hope they spread.

First footing

The first person to enter a home on Christmas morning shouted, "First footing." It was important that the visitor, preferably a dark-haired man or boy, bring something for the household, too, even if it was only a piece of coal for the fire. If he or she failed to bring a gift, unhappiness would befall the family that lived there.

Gifts

Many people believe that the custom of giving Christmas gifts began with God's supreme gift of His Son to the world. Before Christ's birth, however, the custom was practiced in Rome. Roman subjects show-ered olive, myrtle, and laurel boughs, symbols of happiness, love, and good health upon their leaders. Eventually, the leaders began to demand more from their subjects than greenery, and valuable articles such as clothing and jewelry were expected.

Season's greetings

Christmas without cards? Few of us can imagine the absence of holiday greetings and warm wishes from friends and family throughout the world. But, until the mid-1800s, Christmas cards were a privilege of the upper class who could read and write.

In 1843, Henry Cole, British businessman, asked an artist to design a Christmas message that he could send to his friends so he could tell them "A Merry Christmas and a Happy New Year to You" personally.

Mumming

Today's Christmas plays and pageants may well have had their origins in the old folk custom of mumming. The word "mumming" probably came from the German word *mumme,* meaning "a mask," and is defined as "making diversion in disguise." Between Allhallows Eve and Easter (the winter months) during the Middle Ages, figures dressed in disguises and traveled from house to house, bringing good cheer. An old quip describes the season:

"To shorten winter's sadness
See where the nymphs with
    gladness
Disguised all are coming
Right wantonly a-mumming,
With a fal-la-la."

Although mummers' plays vary greatly, the main figures and story line are generally similar. Father Christmas and perhaps a small boy, dressed in a red vest and portraying Robin Redbreast, introduce the play. Then the hero, Saint (or King) George, slays the Turkish Knight, Bold Slasher, and Dragon, who are then restored to life by the Quack Doctor. The revived villains, singing carols, then pass a collection box among the audience. It is believed the story illustrates the magic of spring's rebirth at the winter's solstice. The essential purpose of the costumes was to disguise the mummers' identities, because if the actors were recognized, the luck that they brought was lost.

In some places, mumming became "mumping," or full-fledged begging. Poor old women would go from door to door soliciting gifts. In return for the alms, the mumpers would offer evergreen sprigs for decorating the homes.

Christmas Wish

May your tree
this Christmas
be a pine tree,
spicy-fragrant,
full-needled,
to bring you
new knowledge
of immortality.
May there be
pine cones
on your tree—
abundance
of life.
And nestled
in the branches
may there be
a bird's nest,
old old symbol
of happiness.

—*Elizabeth Searle Lamb*

Christmas Greenery

Long before the Christian era, evergreens symbolized eternal life because, although the bitterly cold winters killed most plants, evergreens survived, a token of summer and life. To ancient pagans, who revered all natural phenomena, the sound of leafy boughs in the breeze wasn't merely the wind; rather, it was the soft voice of the god who dwelled within the tree. Plants such as pine, spruce, holly, ivy, bay, mistletoe, and rosemary were believed to shield them from evil spirits.

Our custom of "decking the halls with boughs of holly" and other types of greenery, might be traced back to the Roman celebration of Saturn, the God of Agriculture. For the festival, held around the 25th of December, Romans filled their homes with greens and gave each other wreaths as a sign of friendship. Early Christians, forced to practice their religion in secret, hung greens on their doors to avoid discovery. The first reference to the Christian use of greens as decorations may have been by Tertullian (A.D. 160-230), a Latin Church father, who said, "You are the light of the world, a tree ever green."

Rosemary

Rosemary can attribute its niche in the Christmas season to its pungent perfume. During the Middle Ages, rosemary was spread on the floor during winter celebrations. When celebrants walked over it, a spicy fragrance was released, which some believed would preserve their youth. When used at weddings, rosemary signified hope, at funerals it signified remembrance.

It's said that rosemary received its fragrance when Mary laid the garments of the Baby Jesus on its branches. Said Sir Thomas More: "'Tis the herb sacred to remembrance and therefore to friendship whence a sprig of it hath a dumb language."

Poinsettia

A native of the American Continent, the poinsettia was discovered in Mexico in 1828 by Dr. Joel Roberts Poinsett, after whom it was named. The Mexicans and people of Central America called the red and green plant *Flor de la Noche Buena* (Flower of the Holy Night) and had their own legend about the poinsettia.

The Legend Of the Poinsettia

In a certain village in Mexico many years ago, it was customary on Christmas Eve to take gifts to the church and place them before the crèche. One evening a small boy went to the church and stood outside the door. How he wished he could enter and present a gift to Jesus, but he was poor. He had nothing to give.

"I can at least pray," he thought to himself. He knelt silently outside the church window and listened to the voices raised in song. When he rose to his feet, he was amazed at what he saw in the spot where he had knelt. It was a beautiful plant with scarlet leaves and a yellow flower in the center. He had never seen anything like it. Realizing it was a miracle, he carefully plucked the flower and took it into the church. As he placed the beautiful flower before the manger, he whispered, "This is my gift to the Christ Child. My own precious gift."

Mistletoe

Nowadays, the mention of mistletoe brings to mind images of stolen kisses under white-berried boughs. How this romantic custom emerged is not known, although some believe it to be a remnant of an ancient marriage rite. Ancient Romans held mistletoe as a symbol of peace. The plant was so sacred that if enemies met beneath a mistletoe-draped tree, they had to lay down their arms and observe a truce until the following day.

Eventually, the custom of hanging mistletoe over doorways came about. Entering signified a pledge of peace and was sealed with a friendly gesture, often a kiss. It also was an invitation to the sprites of the forest to come in out of the cold on long winter nights and bring good cheer and security against jealous gods.

In the old Norse myth of Balder, the god of the summer sun was killed by a mistletoe-tipped spear and then restored to life by his mother Freyja, the goddess of love. Mistletoe is seen as an emblem of that love, a love stronger than death—the same love Christ demonstrated through his suffering on the cross and resurrection.

Holly

It's not surprising that many consider holly the ultimate Christmas plant. As with other evergreens, holly was revered as a symbol of everlasting life. It was used in German church decorations to guard against lightning, ancient warriors chewed it for courage and strength, and Old English maidens put a berried sprig on their beds at night to ward off unwelcome visits from goblins.

As holly became Christianized, its characteristics were thought to depict the history of Christ's life. The red berries became drops of His blood, the white flowers a sign of His purity, the bitter bark symbolic of His suffering, and the sharp pointed leaves emblematic of His crown of thorns.

Ivy

Many old folk songs tell of the rivalry between the ivy, thought to be a female plant, and the holly, thought to be a male plant. Because the ivy was once worn by heathens in honor of the wine-god Bacchus, it was not thought worthy in houses.

In Italy, however, ground ivy was elevated in stature by its association with the Madonna and Child. It was believed that the patches of sweet-smelling, heart-shaped ivy leaves marked *que Dieu Marcha* (where God has walked).

Mistletoe Sprites

Wee sprites have followed mistletoe
Since pagan days of long ago.
In tight soft breeches, dusty green,
The little folk can scarce be seen,
But pearly buttons fasten tight
Their tiny jackets, left and right,
And sometimes on the mistletoe
A bunch of buttons softly glow.
We call them berries, but it's clear
When we see berries, sprites are near.
And wherever these folks go
Good luck comes with mistletoe!

—Solveig Paulson Russell

Festivities Around The World

For nearly two thousand years, millions of people have celebrated Christmas through stories, songs, and fellowship. Take a look at some of the Christmas customs observed in other lands. Perhaps you'll see one or two that will become traditions in your home.

Brazil

Santa Claus is not as popular in Brazil as in many parts of the world, but those who do know him call him *"Papa Noel."* Since fireplaces are not necessary in this warm climate, Santa enters through an open window on Christmas Eve to bring presents to the children.

At the stroke of midnight on Christmas Eve, a legend says, the animals speak. The cock crows, *"Christo nasceu"* (Christ is born). He is answered by the bull, asking, *"Onde?"* (Where?). The sheep then respond by saying, *"Em Belem de Juda"* (In Bethlehem of Judea).

India

Christians raise a Christmas flag in early December to announce the coming holiday. On the evening of Christmas Day, Christian households light candles and display them on their roofs like the stars in the Bethlehem sky.

France

On Christmas Eve, after children have gone off to bed, parents decorate Christmas trees with small toys and candy. Then *Père Noel* quietly enters and puts small gifts in shoes that the children have set out by the fireplace.

Nicaragua

Christmas offically begins in Nicaragua on December 6, although actual activities start on December 16, with performances of the story of Joseph and Mary. Each home has a crèche, and from December 16 to Christmas Eve, mass and prayers, followed by caroling, are held nightly in the home. Christmas cards are exchanged but bear little resemblance to our brightly colored ones. Cards are plain white and say simply: *Felices Pascuas y próspero Año Nuevo* (Happy Christmas and a prosperous New Year).

Ireland

Until recently, groups of singers and dancers celebrated Christmas by going door to door performing songs and jigs from medieval mummers' plays. An especially popular ballad of the day told of a wren, which betrayed St. Stephen to Roman soldiers, and it is still widely sung today.

A common decoration in Irish homes is a large candle placed near a window and lighted on Christmas Eve by the family's youngest member to guide strangers as the star guided the holy family. Though it has a religious meaning now, this tradition can be traced back to Roman times, when candles were lighted at the midwinter festival to symbolize light returning after the winter solstice.

Norway

During the Christmas holiday, Norwegian children dress in costumes and visit homes to ask for treats, just as American children do at Halloween.

The Bird Tree

At Christmas time, especially in very cold places like Scandinavia, birds are given special treats. In Sweden they have what they call the bird tree. This is a wheel that is raised on a tall pole in the farmyard. On the wheel are placed sheaves of corn or wheat for the birds. Handfuls of grain also are placed on windowsills, roofs, and garden walls.

In rural Poland, a sheaf of wheat stands in a corner of every room of the house on Christmas Eve. These are later taken out to the orchard, both as charms to ensure a plentiful harvest and as a feast for the birds.

Australia

In 1937, a Melbourne radio announcer spied an elderly woman sitting alone at an open window with a candle in her hand, singing along with the Christmas carols on her radio.

The woman died before learning she had inspired the broadcaster to gather together people of all beliefs at a local park. Holding lighted candles, several thousand people sang Christmas carols, ending with "Auld Lang Syne."

Now, the tradition of "Candlelight Caroling" has become so popular that people from all walks of life join in the singing celebration at 10 p.m. on Christmas Eve. Since 1950, the program has been broadcast throughout Australia and the world, bringing Christmas joy to millions.

Austria

In accordance with a legend that describes a wonderful transformation of nature at the birth of Christ, when rivers flowed with wine and trees blossomed in the midst of snow and ice, Austrians collect boughs of cherry, pear, or hawthorn in early December. These are then brought inside and placed in wet sand or water, which causes them to bloom at Christmastime.

Japan

For the Japanese, Christmas isn't really a family day because few families are of the Christian belief. Instead, it is a day set aside for Christians to do something for others, mainly the hospitalized. *Meri Kurisumasu* truly means to them Christ coming again into their hearts with new strength to help them go out into the world and serve others.

Iran

Iran, or Persia, is important in Christmas history because it is believed that the three Wise Men or Magi came from this country.

Here, Christmas is known as the "Little Feast" (Easter is the "Great Feast.") The first 25 days of December are spent fasting; no meat, eggs, milk, or cheese is allowed. The people meditate and attend Church services regularly. Then, just before dawn on Christmas Day, the people break the fast and receive Communion.

Gifts are not exchanged nor does Santa visit, but children often receive a new outfit to wear throughout Christmas week.

Feasting On Tradition

Gathering the clan together for Christmas dinner is a cherished holiday tradition in this country. When family members converge on your home this year, give them a taste of history by serving this traditional feast: turkey with all the trimmings.

At left are *Roast Turkey with Sage Stuffing, Mashed Potatoes,* and *Cranberry Sauce.* Recipes are on page 89.

Turkey Roasting Guide

Type of Turkey	Ready-to-Cook Weight	Oven Temp.	Guide to Roasting Time
Stuffed Whole Turkey	6-8 lbs.	325°	3-3½ hrs.
	8-12 lbs.	325°	3½-4½ hrs.
	12-16 lbs.	325°	4-5 hrs.
	16-20 lbs.	325°	4½-5½ hrs.
	20-24 lbs.	325°	5-6½ hrs.
Turkey Breast and Portions	2-4 lbs.	325°	1½-2 hrs.
	3-5 lbs.	325°	1½-2½ hrs.
	5-7 lbs.	325°	2-2½ hrs.

Sage Stuffing

1 cup finely chopped celery
1 medium onion, chopped
    (½ cup)
½ cup butter *or* margarine
1 teaspoon poultry seasoning
    or ground sage
¼ teaspoon salt
⅛ teaspoon pepper
8 cups dry bread cubes
¾ to 1 cup chicken broth *or*
    water

In a saucepan cook celery and onion in butter or margarine till
tender but not brown. Remove
from the heat; stir in poultry seasoning or sage, salt, and pepper.
Place bread cubes in a large mixing bowl. Add celery mixture.
Drizzle with enough broth or water to moisten, tossing lightly. Use
to stuff one 10-pound turkey.
Makes 10 to 12 servings.

Oyster Stuffing: Prepare the
Sage Stuffing as directed above,
except add 1 pint shucked *oysters,*
drained and chopped, *or* two 8-
ounce cans whole *oysters,* drained
and chopped, with seasonings. Reserve drained oyster liquid if desired, and substitute it for part of
the chicken broth or water. Continue as directed above.

Chestnut Stuffing: Prepare
Sage Stuffing as directed above,
except add 1 pound fresh *chestnuts,*
roasted and coarsely chopped, *or*
12 ounces canned unsweetened
chestnuts, coarsely chopped, with
seasonings. Continue as directed.

Mashed Potatoes

6 medium potatoes
    (2 pounds)
2 tablespoons butter *or*
    margarine
¼ teaspoon salt
    Dash pepper
    Milk, heated (about ¼ cup)

Peel and quarter potatoes. In a
saucepan, cook potatoes, covered,
in lightly salted boiling water for
20 to 25 minutes or till tender.
Drain. Mash with a potato mash-
er, or, using an electric mixer on
low speed, mash potatoes. Add
milk, butter or margarine, salt,
and pepper. Continue beating till
light and fluffy. Makes 8 servings.

Mashed Sweet Potatoes: Prepare Mashed Potatoes as above,
except substitute 2 pounds *sweet potatoes* for potatoes.

Cranberry Sauce

1½ cups sugar
1¼ cups water
1 12-ounce package (3 cups)
    cranberries

In a large saucepan combine sugar
and water. Bring to boiling, stirring constantly. Boil, uncovered,
for 3 minutes. Add cranberries;
return to boiling. Cook over high
heat for 8 minutes or till skins pop.
Serve warm or chilled. (For molded sauce, after mixture returns to
boiling, cook for 10 minutes or till
drop of sauce gels on a cold plate.
Turn into a 3-cup mold. Chill till
firm. Unmold.) Makes 2½ cups.

Roast Turkey With Stuffing

1 10-pound turkey
    Sage Stuffing, Oyster
    Stuffing, *or* Chestnut
    Stuffing*
    Cooking oil *or* melted
    butter

Rinse turkey, then pat dry with
paper towels. Season the body
cavity with salt. Loosely spoon
stuffing into the neck cavity; do
not pack. Pull the neck skin over
the stuffing to the back of the bird.
Fasten the neck skin securely to
the back with a small wooden or
metal skewer. Spoon stuffing into
body cavity. Secure legs under
band of skin across the tail or tie to
tail with a string. Twist wing tips
under back.

Place turkey, breast side up, on
a rack in a shallow roasting pan.
Brush skin with oil or melted butter. Insert a meat thermometer in
the center of the inside thigh mus-
cle, making sure the bulb of the
thermometer does not touch the
bone. Cover bird loosely with foil.
Roast turkey in a 325° oven for
3½ to 4 hours or till thermometer
registers 180° to 185°. Uncover
turkey during the last 45 minutes
of roasting.

Cover turkey; let stand for 20
minutes before carving. Makes 10
to 12 servings.

*Note: *Unstuffed* turkeys generally require 30 to 45 minutes less
total roasting time.

The Cratchits' Christmas Dinner

—Charles Dickens

His active little crutch was heard upon the floor, and back came Tiny Tim before another word was spoken, escorted by his brother and sister to his stool before the fire; and while Bob, turning up his cuffs—as if, poor fellow, they were capable of being made more shabby—compounded some hot mixture in a jug with gin and lemons, and stirred it round and round and put it on the hob to simmer; Master Peter, and the two ubiquitous young Cratchits went to fetch the goose, with which they soon returned in high procession.

Such a bustle ensued that you might have thought a goose the rarest of all birds; a feathered phenomenon, to which a black swan was a matter of course—and in truth it was something very like it in that house. Mrs. Cratchit made the gravy (ready beforehand in a little saucepan) hissing hot; Master Peter mashed the potatoes with incredible vigor; Miss Belinda sweetened up the apple-sauce; Martha dusted the hot plates; Bob took Tiny Tim beside him in a tiny corner at the table; the two young Cratchits set chairs for everybody, not forgetting themselves, and mounting guard upon their posts, crammed spoons into their mouths, lest they should shriek for goose before their turn came to be helped. At last the dishes were set on, and grace was said. It was succeeded by a breathless pause, as Mrs. Cratchit, looking slowly all along the carving-knife, prepared to plunge it in the breast; but when she did, and when the long-expected gush of stuffing issued forth, one murmur of delight arose all round the board, and even Tiny Tim, excited by the two young Cratchits, beat on the table with the handle of his knife, and feebly cried Hurrah!

There never was such a goose. Bob said he didn't believe there ever was such a goose cooked. Its tenderness and flavor, size and cheapness, were the themes of universal admiration. Eked out by apple-sauce and mashed potatoes, it was a sufficient dinner for the whole family; indeed, as Mrs. Cratchit said with great delight (surveying one small atom of a bone upon the dish), they hadn't ate it all at last! Yet every one had had enough, and the youngest Cratchits in particular, were steeped in sage and onion to the eyebrows! But now, the plates being changed by Miss Belinda, Mrs. Cratchit left the room alone—too nervous to bear witness—to take the pudding up and bring it in.

Suppose it should not be done enough! Suppose it should break in turning out! Suppose somebody should have got over the wall of the back-yard, and stolen it, while they were merry with goose—a supposition at which the two young Cratchits became livid! All sorts of horrors were supposed.

Hallo! A great deal of steam! The pudding was out of the copper. A smell like a washing-day! That was the cloth. A smell like an eating-house and a pastrycook's next door to each other, with a laundress's next door to that! That was the pudding! In half a minute Mrs. Cratchit entered—flushed, but smiling proudly—with the pudding, like a speckled cannon-ball, so hard and firm, blazing in half of half-a-quartern of ignited brandy, and bedight with Christmas holly stuck into the top.

Oh, a wonderful pudding! Bob Cratchit said, and calmly too, that he regarded it as the greatest success achieved by Mrs. Cratchit since their marriage. Mrs. Cratchit said that now the weight was off her mind, she would confess she had had her doubts about the quantity of flour. Everybody had something to say about it, but nobody

said or thought it was at all a small pudding for a large family. It would have been flat heresy to do so. Any Cratchit would have blushed to hint at such a thing.

At last the dinner was all done, the cloth was cleared, the hearth swept, and the fire made up. The compound in the jug being tasted, and considered perfect, apples and oranges were put upon the table, and a shovelful of chestnuts on the fire. Then all the Cratchit family drew round the hearth, in what Bob Cratchit called a circle, meaning half a one; and at Bob Cratchit's elbow stood the family display of glass. Two tumblers, and a custard-cup without a handle.

These held the hot stuff from the jug, however, as well as golden goblets would have done; and Bob served it out with beaming looks, while the chestnuts on the fire sputtered and cracked noisily. Then Bob proposed:

"A Merry Christmas to us all, my dears. God bless us!" Which all the family re-echoed.

"God bless us every one!" said Tiny Tim, the last of all. ♣

Christmas Puddings

Warm, spicy, steamed puddings filled with fruit and nuts have been part of the Christmas feast for nearly 400 years. They date to the Roman conquest of much of Britain.

At that time, the thick, sweet-sour grain or vegetable soups, or pottages, were daily fare. They simmered slowly in large pots over open wood fires.

By the Middle Ages, wealthy people were adding meat or fish, dried fruits, and sugar or honey to their pottage. Some of these dishes were thickened with bread crumbs and egg yolks, as well.

Fancy French dishes later pushed these pottages from favor, although the "stewed broth" survived. In about 1420, the broth was said to be a standing pottage, made with veal, chicken, or mutton, thickened with bread and rich with currants.

Some time later, dried plums were added to the stewed broth and the name evolved to plum pottage. Eventually, the plums were replaced by currants and raisins, and remained only in the names. Plum pottage had become a part of the Christmas dinner by about 1600, but as a *first course,* followed by an abundant feast.

Pottage to pudding
Still later, increased trade with the West Indies made sugar affordable to middle-income families.

This reduced dependence on spices for flavor enhancement and concealment of off-flavors. As a result, pies and pottages divided into sweet or savory versions of the same dish; the sweet version of plum pottage was refined into today's plum pudding.

In 1675 came the first reference to the steamed cake as plum pudding. By that time the recipe had become so sweet and rich that it was moved to the dessert course of the yuletide meal.

It is possible the term "king size" originated with a gigantic plum pudding made in a Devonshire village in 1714. The villagers presented it to King George I for Christmas dinner, his first as king. The brandy-laced dessert was made of 400 pounds of flour, 120 pounds of suet, and 120 pounds of raisins. The 900-pound finished product was transported to the center of the village by three horses. There the pudding was sliced and served. The villagers were chagrined to discover it was not quite done. Even so, it's said the royal gentleman was appreciative.

Victorian puddings
A picture of the making of plum pudding was described in *The London Illustrated Times* in 1848. "In a household where there are five or six children, the eldest not above ten or eleven, the making of the pudding is indeed an event. It is thought of days, if not weeks, before. To be allowed to share in the noble work is a prize for young ambition. Lo! the lid is raised, curiosity stands on tip-toe, eyes sparkle with anticipation, little hands are clapped in ecstasy, almost too great to find expression in words.

"The hour arrives—the moment wished and feared. And then when it is dished, when all fears are over, when the roast beef has been removed, when the pudding in all the glory of its own splendour shines upon the table, how eager is the anticipation of the near delight! How delicious it smells! How round it is! A kiss is round, the horizon is round, the earth is round, the moon is round, the sun and stars, and the host of heaven are round. So is plum pudding.''

During Queen Victoria's reign in the late 19th century, plum puddings reached the peak of their popularity. The royal family celebrated Christmas sumptuously, and plum pudding became a part of the season for every family who could possibly afford it.

In Victorian times, plum pudding was cooked slowly and for a long time to allow the shortening (suet) to melt and be dispersed throughout the pudding. If it cooked too quickly, the pudding would be solid and hard. According to a maxim of the day, the dessert was to cook for three days and ripen for three weeks.

Some people cooked their puddings one Christmas and stored them until the next. The method was challenged in the 1857 edition of *Miss Leslie's New Cookery Book.* ''However long they may be preserved from absolute decomposition, these things are always best when fresh.'' Six weeks was the maximum time she recommended storing the product.

Customs and charms
In England, a host of beliefs and superstitions grew up around the making and serving of Christmas pudding.

The Collect read in the Church of England on the last Sunday before Advent begins with the words, ''Stir up, we beseech Thee . . . .'' The phrase came to be regarded as an admonition to start the Christmas pudding at once. Each family member, eyes closed, took a turn stirring the pudding mixture and made a wish.

As the batter was mixed, a ring, a coin, a thimble, and a button, each wrapped in paper so they could be seen and not be swallowed by accident, were added. It was said that whoever found the ring in their serving on Christmas day would be married in the coming year. The coin denoted wealth; the thimble, spinsterhood; and the button, bachelorhood.

Charles Dickens described vividly a 19th-century English Christmas dinner and its plum pudding climax in *A Christmas Carol.* (See ''The Cratchit's Christmas Dinner,'' pages 90 and 91.)

The plum pudding of Dickens' day was rich and heavy with suet, bread crumbs, dried fruits, and spices, but no plums. The standard cooking method, until about 1900, was boiling the pudding mixture in a cloth. The muslin cloth was dipped in boiling water, then floured. The batter was placed in the center and the cloth gathered around it, giving the pudding the cannonball shape.

As American as plum pudding
It was the early settlers from England who brought the pudding tradition to the southern colonies. The first colonists in New England were the Puritans, whose strict religion decried Christmas festivities and everything connected with them as pagan. Not until several generations later did plum pudding find its place on holiday tables there. ♠

Yule! Yule!
Three puddings in a pool;
Crack nuts and cry Yule!

—*Anonymous*

Mocha Steamed Pudding

- 3 slices white bread, torn
- ¾ cup milk
- 2 eggs
- ¾ cup sugar
- 1 teaspoon instant coffee crystals
- ¼ cup cooking oil
- 1 cup all-purpose flour
- ¼ cup unsweetened cocoa powder
- 2 teaspoons baking powder
- 1 cup raisins, chopped
- ½ cup chopped walnuts
  Coffee-Butter Sauce

Combine bread and milk; let stand for 5 to 10 minutes. Beat with a mixer till well mixed. Beat in eggs and sugar. Dissolve coffee crystals in ¼ cup *hot water.* Stir coffee mixture and oil into bread. Combine flour, cocoa, baking powder, and ¼ teaspoon *salt.* Stir into bread mixture; fold in raisins and nuts.

Pour batter into a well-greased 1½-quart mold. Cover with foil; tie with string. Place on a rack in a deep kettle; add boiling water to kettle to a depth of 1 inch. Cover kettle; steam about 2 hours or till done. Add more boiling water as necessary. Cool for 10 minutes. Unmold. Serve with Coffee-Butter Sauce. Serves 8 to 10.

Coffee-Butter Sauce: In a small mixer bowl beat ½ cup *butter or margarine* for 30 seconds. Gradually add 2 cups sifted *powdered sugar.* Beat till light and fluffy. Beat in 2 tablespoons *coffee liqueur* and 1 teaspoon *vanilla.*

Hard Sauce

- ½ cup butter *or* margarine
- 1 cup sifted powdered sugar
- 2 tablespoons whipping cream
- ½ teaspoon shredded lemon peel
- ½ teaspoon vanilla
- 1 cup sifted powdered sugar

In a medium mixer bowl beat together butter or margarine, 1 cup sifted powdered sugar, whipping cream, shredded lemon peel, and vanilla with an electric mixer on medium speed. Add 1 cup sifted powdered sugar; beat till smooth. Spoon or pipe about 1 tablespoon of mixture into paper or foil bonbon cups. (*Or,* spoon mixture into storage container; cover.) Chill. Makes 1½ cups.

The Christmas Pudding

Into the basin put the plums,
Stirabout, stirabout, stirabout!

Next the good white flour comes,
Stirabout, stirabout, stirabout!

Sugar and peel and eggs and spice,
Stirabout, stirabout, stirabout!

Mix them and fix them
and cook them twice,
Stirabout, stirabout, stirabout!

Regal Plum Pudding

- 3 slices bread, torn into pieces
- 1 5⅓-ounce can evaporated milk
- 2 ounces beef suet, ground
- ¾ cup packed brown sugar
- 1 beaten egg
- ¼ cup orange juice
- ½ teaspoon vanilla
- 1½ cups raisins
- ¾ cup snipped pitted dates
- ½ cup diced mixed candied fruits and peels
- ⅓ cup chopped walnuts
- ¾ cup all-purpose flour
- 1½ teaspoons ground cinnamon
- ¾ teaspoon baking soda
- ¾ teaspoon ground cloves
- ¾ teaspoon ground mace
  Hard Sauce

In a large bowl soak bread in milk about 3 minutes or till softened; beat lightly to break up. Stir in suet, brown sugar, egg, orange juice, and vanilla. Add raisins, dates, candied fruits and peels, and nuts. Stir together flour, cinnamon, soda, cloves, mace, and ¼ teaspoon *salt.* Add to fruit mixture; stir till combined.

Pour batter into a well-greased 6½-cup tower mold. Cover with foil, pressing foil tightly against rim of mold. Place on a rack in a deep kettle; add boiling water to a depth of 1 inch. Cover kettle; steam for 4 hours or till done. Add more boiling water as necessary. Cool for 10 minutes. Unmold. Serve with Hard Sauce. Serves 8 to 10.

Flower of England, fruit of Spain,
Met together in a shower of rain,
Put in a bag and tied with a string,
If you guess the answer, I'll give you a pin.

—*English Riddle*

Answer: A Christmas Pudding

Suzanne's Own Night

—Bess Streeter Aldrich

Christmas Eve of 1855 in the Martins' big log-and-frame house there at the edge of the grove which swept up from the timberland along Iowa's Red Cedar River!

It was very cold. Several settlers had frozen to death in near-by localities, so said the papers. There was a little newspaper in each town now, the *Iowa State Register* in Prairie Rapids, the *Banner* in Sturgis Falls. That was progress for you.

continued

The west windows in the lean-to were packed solid with snow, the east ones only less so by a few square inches of peep-holes. The main room was warm as far as the fire from the four-foot logs could throw its heat. Beyond that it was as cold as though one stepped into another clime. In Sarah's bedroom the frost sparkled on the white-washed logs of the walls. Up the loft ladders the east bedroom was only less cold than the outdoors by the slight advantage given from a roof breaking the sweep of prairie wind. The west loft had one mildly warm spot in it. By standing with one's back flattened against the wall where the fireplace chimney passed through, one could detect a faint response of heat.

But as standing with one's back flattened to a chimney was inconvenient for any protracted period, the inmates of the west chamber were as near to a state of freezing as those of the east. All the girls wore flannel nightgowns, flannel nightcaps, and flannel bedsocks, and rather perilously, with much squealing, carried up the ladders each night pieces of hot soapstone wrapped in fragments of clean worn rugs. Safely up the ladders without having dropped hot stones on whoever came behind, they climbed onto featherbeds, pulled other feather-stuffed ticks and several pieced comforts over them, and if their clattering tongues ceased and their exuberant spirits calmed down sufficiently soon, were not long in going soundly to sleep.

To-night all were around the fireplace except Sabina, who was over in her Sturgis Falls home getting ready her first Christmas dinner for them all on the morrow. Henry and Lucy had come over from the other house so there were still eleven people. Lucy sat in Ma's red-covered rocker out of deference to her delicate condition, a concession that had its humorous side when one stopped to think that all year she had washed, ironed, baked, scrubbed, made soap, hoed in the garden, gone after the cows in the timber, and on occasion helped milk. But this was Christmas Eve and all at once every one was deferential to the Madonna-like potentialities of Lucy.

Christmas Eve was Suzanne's own night. It had been made for her. Sitting on the floor with her back to the edge of the fireplace, arms around her knees while the light played over the room, she had that feeling which always came with this special night. She could not put it into words which satisfied her, but in some vague way knew it was magic—the night for which one lived all year.

In the summer, with the mourning-doves and the bouncing-Bets, the wild grape-vine swings and the long walks in the timber, you forgot entirely the feeling that this night could bring. To think of it gave you no emotion whatever. In the early fall you began to remember it. By November it became a bright light toward which you walked. And now to-night you could not think with one bit of excitement how much you liked the summer things. Yes, it was magic. The snow piled against the window was not like other snows. The wind in the chimney was not like other winds. If you scratched a frosted place out of which to look, you saw that the snow-packed prairie to the north was a white country in which no other person lived, that the snow-packed timberland to the south was a white woods forever silent. It was as though there were no human at all in any direction but your own family. Christmas Eve was a white light that drew a magic circle around the members of your own family to hem them all in and fasten them together.

Every one was laughing and talking there in front of the fire where the long knitted stockings hung. Soon now they would all get up and go after the funny-shaped packages hidden in drawers and under beds and put them in the stockings. Suzanne had something for every one—a little pincushion fitted into a river shell for each girl, a fancy box for Ma, with tiny shells fastened thick on it with glue made from old Rosy's hoofs, handkerchiefs hemmed from an outgrown petticoat for Pa, Phineas, and Henry, a corn-cob doll for—she still felt undecided whether or not it would be quite nice to put a corn-cob doll in Lucy's stocking.

The pale yellow light from the tallow candles on the shelf and the brighter reddish light from the wood logs made all the faces stand out from the darkness behind them.

Something about the magic of this night made the folks seem queer and different, too. You could not tell why, but to-night every poor quality about them fell away and only the good ones remained—Pa's big certainty that his way was always right, Ma's scolding, Henry's stubborn quietness, Phineas' smart-Aleck ways, Emily's freckled homeliness, Jeanie's silly changeableness, Phoebe Lou's teasing, Melinda's rough tomboyishness, Celia's vanity. Her heart warmed to them all.

"I'll never think of those imaginary people again," she told herself. "I'll just stay by my own real folks."

Pa was telling about Christmastime back in England; things his grandfather had told him that had come down in the tales from there—about the piping and dancing, the carols and the maskers and the woodcocks cooked in gin. "My great-grandfather's family was landed gentry back in the mother country. Ma's ancestor hung the light in Old North Church when the British was comin'. Ma says her father told her the man was to hang one light if they come by land and two if they was comin' by sea. Both sides they bore arms for the country, faithful and loyal. You children don't never need to take a back seat for anybody. Just hold up your head and speak up all your lives. Both sides good landed-gentry blood runs in your veins and . . ."

If you listened above the din of the talking you could hear the wind in the chimney turn into music. Christmas Eve was a night of song that wrapped itself about you like a shawl. But it warmed more than your body. It warmed your heart . . . filled it, too, with melody that would last forever. Even though you grew up and found you could never quite bring back the magic feeling of this night, the melody would stay in your heart always—a song for all the years. ♣

O Holy Night

O holy night, the stars are brightly shining;
It is the night of the dear Savior's birth.
Long lay the world in sin and error pining,
Till He appeared and the soul felt its worth.
A thrill of hope, the weary soul rejoices,
For yonder breaks a new and glorious morn.
Fall on your knees,
Oh, hear the angel voices!
O night divine, O night when Christ was born!
O night, O holy night, O night divine!

Led by the light of faith serenely beaming,
With glowing hearts by His cradle we stand.
So led by light of a star sweetly gleaming,
Here came the wise men from the Orient land.
The King of Kings lay in lowly manger,
In all our trials born to be our friend.
He knows our need,
To our weakness no stranger.
Behold your King! before the lowly bend!
Behold your King! your King! before Him bend!

Truly He taught us to love one another;
His law is love and His gospel is peace.
Chains shall He break, for the slave is our brother,
And in His name all oppression shall cease.
Sweet hymns of joy in grateful chorus rise we,
Let all within us praise His holy name.
Christ is the Lord,
Then ever, ever praise we;
His pow'r and glory ever more proclaim,
His pow'r and glory ever more proclaim.

The Promise of the Star

As you begin counting the number of shopping days till Christmas, before the Thanksgiving turkey has even begun to cool, pause for a moment. Amidst the preholiday sales, the dazzling lights, and the messages proclaiming Santa Claus is coming to town, consider a long-ago star and its simple message of hope.

Fact or fable
Halley's comet brought with it last year renewed interest in the Star of Bethlehem and the popular theories about its origin.

One theory is that a comet may have appeared to lead the Wise Men to Bethlehem. Halley's comet appeared about 12 B.C. in the constellation Leo, a symbol of the Lion of Judah, making it a popular candidate in the comet category. However, people of Christ's time believed comets foretold tragedies not triumphs, so it's unlikely that such an appearance would have been regarded so joyously.

Another theory suggests a supernova—a gigantic exploding star that becomes so bright it's visible even during daylight hours. Ancient Chinese astronomers made note of a "large fiery star" that appeared in 6 B.C. and lasted for some time.

Another explanation of the star phenomenon is a planetary conjunction. That's when two planets appear to be very close to each other when they're viewed from the earth. A rare conjunction of three planets—Mars, Saturn, and Jupiter—occurred about 7–6 B.C. in the constellation Pisces. Pisces, the fish, was regarded as symbolic of the House of Israel and the Messiah. As for the planets, Saturn was believed to have special guardianship over Israel's 12 tribes, and Jupiter was thought to have royal status. The unusually bright pattern created by such a conjunction would have held special significance to astrologers like the Wise Men (Magi), perhaps causing them to seek out an explanation of the phenomenon.

And it came to pass
Regardless of the ability of science to determine exactly what it was, the Star of Bethlehem holds deep religious significance for many.

Since the dawn of time, men have gazed toward the heavens in wonderment. In the Near East years ago, the stars were regarded as supernatural beings with the power to affect human destiny.

Throughout the Bible, the Star is a symbol of greatness and of hope for the future. The Star of Bethlehem was seen by Matthew as the fulfillment of Old Testament prophecies telling of a heavenly sign proclaiming the birth of the Messiah.

Star light, star bright
The symbolism of the Star endures yet today in poetry, stories, and songs. In his charming story "The Little Prince," Antoine de Saint Exupéry seemingly parallels the life of Christ through an extraordinary small person from a distant star who came to earth seeking the true meaning of life. Here the Little Prince is speaking to the author:

"All men have the stars . . . but they are not the same things for different people. For some, who are travelers, the stars are guides. For others they are no more than little lights in the sky. For others, who are scholars, they are problems . . . But all these stars are silent. You—you alone—will have the stars as no one else has them."

Wish upon a star
There is something comforting in the constancy and endurance of the heavens in this fragile world. Wherever we are, we can gaze at the friendly, familiar stars overhead and know they hold the power to inspire us. It doesn't matter what exactly the Star of Bethlehem was. The rebirth of hope it brought so long ago is as urgent today as it was yesterday. And, if we hold fast to the promise of the Christmas Star, that hope will be with us in the future. ♠

At Christmas Time

At Christmas time we deck the hall
With holly branches brave and tall,
With sturdy pine and hemlock bright
And in the Yule log's dancing light
We tell old tales of field and fight
At Christmas time.

At Christmas time we pile the board
With flesh and fruit and vintage stored,
And mid the laughter and the glow
We tread a measure soft and slow,
And kiss beneath the mistletoe
At Christmas time.

—traditional English verse

Holiday Favorites

Stories _____
_____
_____
_____

Carols _____
_____
_____
_____

Movies/TV Shows _____
_____
_____
_____

Poems _____
_____
_____
_____

Books _____
_____
_____
_____

Favorite Christmas Memories

_____
_____
_____
_____
_____
_____
_____
_____
_____
_____
_____
_____
_____
_____
_____
_____
_____
_____
_____
_____
_____
_____
_____
_____
_____
_____
_____
_____
_____

What Christmas Means to Me

Holiday Entertaining

Type of get-together, guest list, activities, food served

_____

_____

_____

_____

_____

_____

_____

_____

_____

_____

_____

_____

_____

_____

_____

_____

_____

_____

_____

_____

_____

_____

_____

_____

_____

_____

_____

_____

Special Moments to Treasure

Photos and other holiday memorabilia

GATHERING
THE
FAMILY

It's not just the sights of Christmas
That make it mean so much;
It's visits of friends and families and
The sounds and the smells and the touch.

—from To Louis at Christmas *by Ilien Coffey*

White Christmas

—Alice Dalgliesh

Marylee Marie lived in the neatest farmhouse on the shore of St. Mary's Bay. The house was very white and green with tall pink geraniums looking out of every window. The woodpile was the longest and most carefully stacked of all the woodpiles from Digby to Tiverton and even the rosy apples on the trees looked as if they had just been scrubbed.

In the summertime, Marylee Marie liked to feed the chickens, to bring the cows home from pasture, and to ride, perched high on her father's blue hay wagon. In the winter it was lonely in the farmhouse which stood by itself quite a distance from any village. The only interesting thing that happened on long winter days was the arrival of the mail bus from Digby. When the bus came Marylee Marie would run out to get the mail bag and to talk to Jim, the driver. Every one liked Jim, for he was always friendly and cheerful, always singing or whistling. Usually his seat in the bus was surrounded by small packages which might be shoes for the young Browns, a kettle for Miss Letty at Sandy Cove, or any sort of strange thing that people asked him to buy for them.

In December just before Marylee Marie's seventh Christmas, the mail bus brought her a letter from her aunt in Boston. The letter said:

"Dear Marylee Marie:

"This is the first year you have had electric light in the farmhouse, so I am going to send you some colored lights for your Christmas tree. Some day next week Jim will bring them to you on the bus."

After that Marylee Marie could hardly wait for the days to go by. They seemed to go very slowly. At last it was three days before Christmas—but still the lights had not come. That morning Marylee's father said:

"Marylee Marie, if we are going to have a Christmas tree we must get it today. Storm warnings are out, and, with the snow that is already here, it looks as though we'd have a real old-fashioned white Christmas."

So Marylee Marie put on her warm blue coat, her red cap, her scarf and rubber boots, and started out with her father. Although there were trees growing near their own gate they went far up the hill to the pasture, for they were looking for a tree that would be quite perfect in shape. It was very still among the trees. Sometimes a chickadee called "Chick-a-dee-dee-dee!" or a tiny red squirrel chattered at them from a branch overhead. Most of the time the only sound was the crunch of crisp snow under rubber boots.

By the far pasture bars they found the tree, a slim, fragrant balsam. Marylee's father cut it down with his sharp ax, and they turned homewards, carrying the tree between them and walking in the tracks they had made before. Through the kitchen door they carried the tree.

"What a beautiful fir," said Marylee's mother, "all trimmed with icicles already. It seems too bad to have to melt them. Put it here by the stove to thaw out."

The tree lay by the stove for an hour or two, and Marylee mopped up the puddles made by melting icicles. At last even the biggest icicle had thawed, and a delightful Christmas tree smell filled the warm kitchen. Then the tree was set at the window of the dining-room looking out across the wintry water of Saint Mary's Bay.

"If only the lights would come!" said Marylee Marie.

By this time snow was falling fast and the wind was rising. All night long it snowed and by morning the wind had become a gale. It blew the snow against the house with little sharp shrieks of fury as if it were trying to blow right through the sturdy walls. That afternoon the bus did not come from Digby.

continued

"Oh!" said Marylee Marie. "Now the lights won't be here in time for Christmas!" She stood by the window of the front parlor looking out at the road through whirling snowflakes. An ox sled went by, slowly and with difficulty, the oxen holding their heads low, snow caked on their broad sides.

"Oh, dear!" said Marylee Marie.

"Don't fret about the lights," said her mother. "Come and help me pack this box for the McLeans. They won't have much of a Christmas unless we make it for them." Marylee forgot her troubles then and scurried around trying to find something for each of the McLean children; the McLeans had so many children, and so little money. It was hard to find something for every one but surprising how many things proved to be tucked away in bureau drawers or in the old trunk under the bed. The baby's present came out of the old trunk, it was a red knitted cap that had belonged to Marylee Marie, a nice round cap with a ribbon rosette on each side. There was a small blue wagon for the older baby, red scarves for the four-year-old twins, a boat for Tim who was six, and dolls for Margery and Jean. The dolls also belonged to Marylee Marie and it took quite a long time to get them ready. Marylee scrubbed their faces and combed their hair while her mother washed and ironed their clothes. When the dolls looked clean and respectable there was a present for every one except twelve-year-old John.

"I think we shall have to give John your father's second-best knife," said Marylee's mother. "I shall put in one of your father's ties for Mr. McLean, and this pretty string of blue beads for Mrs. McLean. Then we can fill the top of the box with candy, nuts, and cookies."

Marylee and her mother wrapped all the gifts in gay papers and tied them with ribbons that had been carefully saved from packages of the year before. Then Marylee put a piece of bright red paper over the top of the box and her mother tied it with stout cord. It was all ready when John McLean came in at the back door, stamping the snow off his boots and wiping it from his eyelashes. He grinned, lifted the box to his shoulder, and tramped off into the snow.

"Tell your mother we'll have a couple of chickens ready for her if she'll send over for them tomorrow," called Marylee's mother.

On Christmas Eve the snow had stopped falling. The sun came out and the steel-gray water of Saint Mary's Bay changed to a deep, cold blue. Each fir tree was trimmed for Christmas. The trees and houses cast blue shadows on the snow. Against the farmhouse fence the drifts were deep and rounded like great feather beds, so soft and inviting that Marylee longed to jump into the middle of them. The day went by, slowly, slowly, and at last it was time for the mail. Marylee Marie stood at the gate between two snowdrifts and looked along the white, lonely road. There was the sound of sleigh bells and around the corner came a large sled drawn by two horses. It was the mail, Marylee knew that, for she could hear Jim's familiar, cheerful voice:
"Noël, Noël, Noël, Noël
Born is the King of Israel."

The sled stopped by the farmhouse gate, then Jim jumped down and handed a large package to Marylee Marie. She hurried into the house with it, just as her mother came out with a cup of hot cocoa for Jim. Marylee put the package on the floor near the Christmas tree and began to tug excitedly at the string. Soon all the wrappings were removed, and she lifted the cover from a cardboard box. Inside, there were packages of all shapes and sizes. First came two boxes of lights for the tree—Marylee was quite disappointed in those because they looked rather uninteresting. Then there were packages of tinsel and other trimmings—Marylee could scarcely believe her eyes when she saw the white woolly sheep with red ribbons around their necks, the small spotted horses with perky tails, and the gay birds to perch on the tips of the branches. Best of all there was a smiling wax angel with very pink cheeks, gauzy wings, and golden hair—she was for the top of the tree.

"Let's trim it right away!" said Marylee Marie.

It was fun to find places for everything and in a short time the little tree sparkled with tinsel and shone with rainbow-colored trimmings. Then came the great moment when Marylee's father connected the lights. The tree blossomed magically, the tinsel was no longer silver but hung in glittering strands of blue and red and gold. Marylee Marie sat on the floor, looking up at the beautiful thing. There is no telling how long she would have sat there if suppertime and bedtime had not come along. Of course Marylee remembered to hang up a red stocking before she went to bed.

Christmas Day came with packages and a bulging stocking for Marylee Marie. There was the Christmas dinner, with so much duck and plum pudding that afterwards every one sat very quietly for a long time. Just as it was growing dark there came the sound of bells, not the gay tinkling bells of a horse sleigh but the slow, dignified bells of an ox sled. The sled stopped at the gate and out tumbled the six McLean children. They raced to the house, shouting, "Thank you for our Christmas box!" and Mr. McLean followed carrying the baby. Marylee's mother opened the door, and the whole family filed through the kitchen. They got no farther than the door of the dining-room, for there they saw the lighted Christmas tree and stood as if rooted to the floor. For a few minutes no one moved or said a word. Then the fat baby started forward on unsteady legs, holding out one red-mittened hand.

"Kismus tee!" she said.

After that all the children crowded around the tree and touched the trimmings with timid exploring fingers.

"O-o-oh, look at the baby lambs!"

"Can't I make the green bird sit on another branch?"

"Looky here at Santy Claus!"

"Look at the fairy!"

"Angel," corrected Marylee Marie. She turned the lights on and off several times, so that they twinkled and seemed more wonderful than ever. Then her mother came in with a plate of cookies and the seven McLeans sat around the tree and looked and munched.

When every one was quite full of cookies, Marylee's mother called the children over to the parlor organ to sing some Christmas hymns. The little parlor organ was slightly out of tune but that did not matter in the least. The six McLeans sang in shrill clear voices, the twins a little behind the others. When the baby began to grow tired of listening, Mr. McLean tucked her under his arm and bundled the children out-of-doors and into the sled.

Marylee stood at the window and watched them go. "Ding, dong!" went the bells. Star and Bright plodded along, fat and placid, paying no attention to the sled full of wriggling, shouting children. The sled grew smaller in the distance, it turned the corner and was out of sight.

Christmas Day was over. Supper was not important, bedtime was welcome. The little tree stood in the window, its lights twinkling out across the snow. Only the gulls that flew over Saint Mary's Bay could see it, for Marylee Marie was fast asleep under three warm layers of patchwork quilt. ♣

Marbleized Ornaments

Just like magic, plain Christmas tree trims
are transformed into treasures when you use this
simple marbleizing technique.

MATERIALS
Glass ornaments
Assorted colors of spray paint
(white, gold metallic, and
either red, blue, green, or
yellow)
Short lengths of ½-inch-diameter
dowel
Small bucket
Stirring stick
Clear acrylic spray

INSTRUCTIONS
To begin, choose a well-venti-
lated area; cover all work surfaces
with newspapers.

Fill a bucket with water to within 2 inches of the rim. Holding a
paint can 8 inches from the water,
spray metallic, white, and one other color of paint onto the water at
a 35-degree angle, spraying each
for four to five seconds. Overlap
the colors slightly on the water.

Slip a dowel into a ball ornament and tape the neck of the ornament to the dowel. Then,
immerse the ornament, slowly ro-
tating it through the paint, rather
than dunking it into the water.
The paint will form a skin on top
of the water. Pushing the skin
away from the ornament with a
stick, remove the ornament. Sus-
pend it until it's dry (about 20
minutes).

Clean the paint away from the
water by collecting it on a stirring
stick and wiping it onto a rag. Repeat the procedure for each ornament. Spray dried ornaments with
clear acrylic.

Stitch-and-Stuff Ornaments

With these pretty ornament designs, Christmas crafting can become a family event. Supply your children with fabric crayons and paints so they can add touches of colors to the fabric ornaments.

MATERIALS
Graph paper
Muslin or white
    lightweight
    cotton fabric
Brown fine-point
    permanent marker
Fiberfill
Short lengths of ribbon
Any or all of the
    following materials for
    decorating the
    ornaments: fabric dye,
    fabric paints,
    embroidery floss,
    embroidery hoop,
    needle, scraps of
    fabric, bugle beads,
    quilting thread,
    colored pencils, fabric
    crayons, ribbon, lace,
    buttons
Purchased appliqués
Batting

INSTRUCTIONS

General directions
To make the ornaments, enlarge the patterns, page 123, onto graph paper, or take the designs to a photo duplication service and have them enlarged professionally. This is fast (often while you wait), but it can be costly.

Once the patterns are enlarged, transfer them to fabric by placing them under the muslin or lightweight cotton fabric. Trace the design lines with a fine-point permanent marker. Be sure to leave at least 1 inch between the ornaments for seam margins.

Decorating the trims
Once the designs are transferred, iron the fabric on the wrong side to heat-set the ink.

Designs then may be embellished with paints, fabric dye, beading, quilting, embroidery, or appliqué. Always decorate the designs before stitching.

FABRIC DYE: To add background color, dip the fabric in a diluted dyebath. (Test the dye on a scrap of fabric before dipping an entire piece.) The color should be light enough for printed or hand-drawn lines to be clearly visible. Use tinted fabric as is or embellish it with embroidery, beading, appliqué, or quilting.

PAINTING: Use high-quality acrylic or fabric paints. Always decorate the designs before assembling the ornaments.

Place a small amount of paint on a glass plate and thin it with a few drops of water until the paint is the consistency of light cream. Make certain the color is light enough for the design lines to be clearly visible.

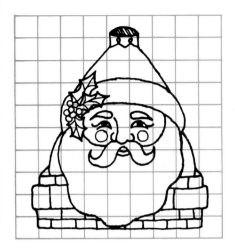

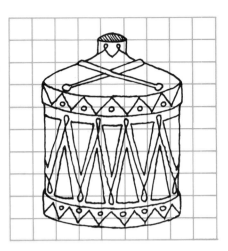

Place fabric designs on several layers of newspaper or paper towels. Dip a small brush into paint; remove excess by lightly dabbing brush on a paper towel. Do not place too much paint on brush.

Beginning with large areas of the design, paint up to the outlines. Leave a sliver of space between color areas. Allow a painted area to dry before working on adjacent areas. When fabric is dry, gently press wrong side with a warm iron to heat-set the paint.

You also may use colored pencils, crayons, and fabric markers to decorate the fabric. Or choose fine-tip permanent marking pens that will not bleed on the fabric or cause the brown outlines to bleed. For best results, use light pen colors since the ink often looks darker when it's applied to fabric.

Once the fabric is colored, heat-set it by pressing it on the wrong side with a warm iron.

Embroidery, by hand or machine, may be used alone or in combination with paint. Use simple stitches and a variety of cotton, silk, and metallic threads for embellishing the designs. Or, use straight, zigzag, or decorative sewing-machine embroidery stitches.

APPLIQUÉS AND BEADS: Motifs may be enhanced with ribbon, lace, buttons, fabric flowers and leaves, purchased appliqués, and lengths of rayon bias tape.

Or, accent design elements with purchased beads. To outline with beads, first thread them onto a single strand of quilting thread. With a second needle threaded with ecru thread, tack the strand between already-strung beads along the printed design line.

QUILTING: Once decorated, the ornaments may be quilted. Sandwich a layer of quilt batting between the decorated fabric and a lightweight backing fabric; quilt along the design lines.

Assembling the projects

When the designs are decorated, cut out the ornaments, leaving ½ inch of fabric outside the outer design lines. Cut matching backs from muslin or fabric scraps. With right sides facing, stitch the fronts and backs together ⅛ inch outside the outer design lines, following curves as closely as possible. Leave openings for turning.

Trim seams, clip curves, notch seam allowances, and turn ornaments right side out. Stuff with fiberfill; slip-stitch openings closed. Attach ribbons for hanging.

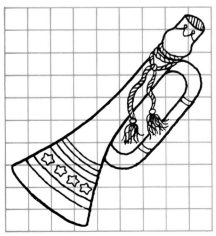

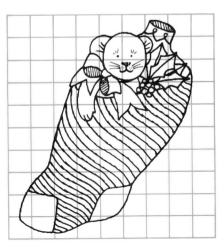

1 Square = ½ Inch

Country Christmas Trims

Spruce up your tree this year with a country
Christmas spirit, using these festive
ornament ideas. You'll find that all three projects
are quick and easy to make.

Cross-Stitch Ornaments

Finished size is 2¾x5 inches.

MATERIALS
5x8-inch pieces of 14-count Aida
  cloth
Scraps of Size 5 pearl cotton in
  various colors
Fiberfill
Wool fabric
Satin ribbon

INSTRUCTIONS
The chart, *right,* gives the pattern for one-fourth of the border. Flopping this pattern, stitch the complete border, using a different color for each symbol. Center and stitch the greeting of your choice.

Cut a wool backing the same size as the cross-stitched front. Sew the backing to the front, right sides together, leaving an opening for turning. Turn, stuff, and hang with a ribbon bow.

Wheat Bundle Ornaments

MATERIALS
Ornamental wheat (sold in crafts
  or florist's shops)
Florist's wire
Red ribbon

INSTRUCTIONS
Aligning the heads of the wheat, gather about a dozen stalks. Fan the heads and wire the stalks together tightly with florist's wire about 3 inches from heads. Trim the ends of the stalks evenly; add ribbon bows and hang from ribbon loops.

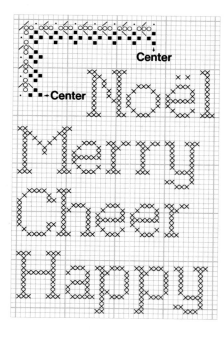

Wooden Heart Ornaments

Finished size is 2½ inches tall.

MATERIALS
½-inch-thick pine
Red acrylic paint
Paintbrush
Sandpaper
Monofilament or ribbon
Drill
Jigsaw
Soft cloth

INSTRUCTIONS
Using a jigsaw, cut out 2½-inch-tall hearts from the pine. Sand the surfaces smooth. Dilute the paint and apply it to the hearts.

While the paint is still wet, wipe the ornaments with a soft cloth to create a stained look. Let dry.

Drill a hole at the top of each ornament. Thread monofilament or ribbon through the hole to hang the ornament.

The Christmas Tree Lamb

—Kathryn Jackson

Once upon a time there was a small, white, Christmas tree lamb. He belonged to a grandmother when she was a little girl. He belonged to a mother, too, when she was small.

And when he belonged to the grandmother, he was a brand-new lamb. His fleece was snowy white against the dark branches of the tree. His black bead eyes shone with lights and excitement. And his shining hooves looked as if he might frolic from branch to branch the very next minute. Besides all that, the tiny golden bell on his collar jingled merrily whenever anyone brushed against the tree.

That was splendid, that first Christmas.

The lamb was new. And the grandmother was little. And everyone said, "The lamb is the prettiest thing on the whole tree!"

There were lots of splendid Christmases.

But after a while, the lamb began to look dusty. After a while the grandmother was grown up. Then the Christmas lamb belonged to the mother.

She loved that lamb when she was little. She played with him every year before she put him on the tree.

And one year, pop! one bead eye came loose and rolled into a corner.

The next year, crack! the Christmas lamb lost a leg.

Three years later, his tiny golden bell fell off, and was lost with the lost things of Christmas.

By the time the mother was grown up and had a little girl of her own, that lamb was in a sorry state! He was gray with dust, and he had but one eye, two legs, no collar, and of course, no bell. But he was still a Christmas lamb, eagerly waiting to go on the tree.

The grandmother picked him up and said, "We can't put him on the tree any more!"

The mother took him and said, "No, he's nothing to look at now. But how pretty he was, long ago!"

Now the little girl reached out her hands for the lamb. "How did he look?" she asked.

The grandmother told about his snowy white fleece.

The mother told about the golden bell that had jingled so merrily.

And the little girl could see for herself that a lamb should have *two* black eyes and *four* shining hooves.

So she took the lamb into her own room. She brushed and cleaned him until he was as white as the snow falling outside. She made him two new legs, and glued them on, and painted them shining black. She sewed a small black bead in place for an eye. And she tied a bit of red ribbon around the snowy lamb's neck, with a new little golden bell in front.

When Christmas Eve came, the little girl crept downstairs with the lamb held behind her back.

She waited until the grandmother wasn't looking. She waited until the mother wasn't looking.

Then she stood on a chair, and put the lamb on the Christmas tree, up near the top, right under the shining star.

When the grandmother saw the lamb, her eyes glistened. "He looks just as he did when I was a little girl," she said in a whisper.

The mother looked then, and her eyes sparkled. "He looks much finer than he did when I was little!" she said.

The little girl didn't say a word.

She was too busy loving the lamb and thinking he was the prettiest thing on the tree. She touched the tree, and the lamb swayed to and fro. His two eyes shone with lights and excitement. His four hooves looked ready to caper from branch to branch.

And his new golden bell jingled more merrily than the old one ever had. Perhaps that was because the small, white Christmas tree lamb was happier than he had ever been in all his white cotton years on all the Christmas trees! ♣

Merry Christmas

In the rush of the merry morning,
When the red burns through the gray,
And the wintry world lies waiting
For the glory of the day;
Then we hear a fitful rushing
Just without upon the stair,
See two white phantoms coming,
Catch the gleam of sunny hair.

Are they Christmas fairies stealing
Rows of little socks to fill?
Are they angels floating hither
With their message of good-will?
What sweet spell are these elves weaving,
As like larks they chirp and sing?
Are these palms of peace from heaven
That these lovely spirits bring?

Rosy feet upon the threshold,
Eager faces peeping through,
With the first red ray of sunshine,
Chanting cherubs come in view;
Mistletoe and gleaming holly,
Symbols of a blessed day,
In their chubby hands they carry,
Streaming all along the way.

Well we know them, never weary
Of this innocent surprise;
Waiting, watching, listening always
With full hearts and tender eyes,
While our little household angels,
White and golden in the sun,
Greet us with the sweet old welcome,—
"Merry Christmas, every one!"

—*Anonymous*

Stocking Stuffers

Gone are the days when a tangerine in the toe of a Christmas stocking would bring delight to the eyes of an eager treasure seeker on Christmas morning. Now the challenge is to stuff stockings with useful, unique, or yearned-for goodies. The key to the challenge is simple: Think small, sizewise and costwise. Then consider each person you must buy for—what they do, what they like, and what they wear.

Work Easers

Fill an executive's stocking with a pen or framed family photo. For the road traveler, choose a cup holder, flashlight, or utility gloves for pumping gas. A homemaker can use a memo pad, egg timer, or kitchen magnets. A pocket calendar, colored pens and pencils, and plastic rulers are sure to please students. Anyone old enough to tell time will value one of those half-dollar-size stick-on clocks for a car, desk, or refrigerator.

Hobbies

Give the amateur carpenter a screwdriver, a wrench, pliers, or paint-mixing sticks. For the gardener, plant a few seed packets, some gardening gloves, or a digging tool in his or her stocking. Sports fans will thank you for golf tees, Ping-Pong balls, fishing lures, a sweatband, or a sun visor.

Cater to the whims of an avid cook with a mushroom brush, pasta measurer, meat thermometer,

or large-size recipe cards. Surprise a music fan with a cassette tape of a favorite recording artist or group. Delight the kids with a new box of crayons, bike-handle tassles, jacks, kazoos, fun-shape straws, squirt guns, a bottle of bubbles, or tiny cars or dolls. And if you know what someone collects, be it charms, cookie cutters, or pennants, your job is a cinch.

Novelties

Browse the aisles of any gift shop and you'll spot creative sundries for everyone: colored paper clips, stickers in every shape and color under the sun, plastic wind-up toys that walk or jump, daily vitamin dispensers, or monogrammed clothespins for identifying anything from towels to sack lunches. Don't worry about unique gifts becoming obsolete with time. This year's novelties may well become next year's necessities.

Grooming Needs

The women on your list will love a bar of scented soap for luxurious bathing. Or tuck in some totable cosmetic items such as a nail file, purse-size make-up mirror, or miniature bottles of cologne. For the guys, a sturdy pocket comb or a tube of lip moistener makes a welcome gift.

Accessories

Fill stockings fashionably with silky scarves or sashes, tie tacks, belts, decorative shoelaces, colorful socks, costume jewelry, and barrettes, combs, and ribbons.

Staples

Save someone you love the trouble of buying such insignificant but indispensable items as books of postage stamps, return-address labels, books of matches, camera film, thumbtacks, masking or transparent tape, scouring pads, flashlight batteries, and small plastic containers for storing or toting.

Edibles

Here are a few delectable suggestions: stuffed olives, squeezable cheese for crackers, small jars of jam, beef jerky, granola bars, trail mix, dried apricots or figs, macadamia or other nuts, chocolate-covered anything, mints, herbal teas, or flavored coffees. ♠

The Christmas Cake

—Maud Lindsay

It was a joyful day for the McMulligan children when Mrs. McMulligan made the Christmas cake. There were raisins to seed and eggs to beat, and pans to scrape, and every one of the children, from the oldest to the youngest, helped to stir the batter when the good things were mixed together.

"Oh, mix it, and stir it, and stir it and taste;
For ev'rything's in it, and nothing to waste;
And ev'ry one's helped—even Baby—
  to make
The nice, brown, sugary Christmas cake,"

said Mrs. McMulligan, as she poured the batter into the cake pan.

The Baker who lived at the corner was to bake the Christmas cake, so Joseph, the oldest boy, made haste to carry it to him. All the other children followed him, and together they went, oh, so carefully, out the front door, down the sidewalk, straight to the shop where the Baker was waiting for them.

The Baker's face was so round and so jolly that the McMulligan children thought he must look like Santa Claus. He could bake the whitest bread and the lightest cake, and as soon as the children spied him they began to call:

"The cake is all ready! 'Tis here in the pan;
Now bake it, good Baker as fast as you can";
"No, no," said the Baker, "'Twould be a
  mistake
To hurry in baking the Christmas cake.
I'll not bake it fast, and I'll not bake it slow;
My little round clock on the wall there will
  show
How long I must watch and how long I must
  bake
The nice, brown, sugary Christmas cake."

The little round clock hung on the wall above the oven. Its face was so bright, and its tick was so merry, and it was busy night and day telling the Baker when to sleep and when to eat and when to do his baking. When the McMulligan children looked at it, it was just striking ten, and it seemed to them very plainly to say:

" 'Tis just the right time for the Baker to bake
The nice, brown, sugary Christmas cake."

The oven was ready, and the Baker made haste to put the cake in.

"Ho, ho," he cried gayly, "now isn't this fun?
'Tis ten by the clock, and the baking's begun,
And tickity, tickity, when it strikes one,
If nothing should hinder the cake will be
  done."

Then the McMulligan children ran home to tell their mother what he had said, and the Baker went on with his work. It was the day before Christmas, and a great many people came to his shop to buy pies and cakes, but no matter how busy he was, waiting on them, he never forgot the McMulligans' cake, and every time he looked at the clock, it reminded him to peep into the oven.

So well did he watch it, and so carefully did he bake it, that the cake was done on the stroke of one, just as he had promised, and he had scarcely taken it out of the oven when the shop door flew open; and in came the McMulligan children, every one of them saying:

"The clock has struck one. The clock has
  struck one.
We waited to hear it—and is the cake done?"

When they saw it they thought it was the nicest, brownest, spiciest cake that was ever baked in a Baker's oven. The Baker himself said it was a beautiful cake, and if you had been at the McMulligans' on Christmas Day, I am sure you would have thought so too.

Joseph carried it home, walking very slowly and carefully, and all the other children followed him, out of the Baker's shop, down the sidewalk, straight home, where Mrs. McMulligan was waiting for them. She was smiling at them from the window, and when they spied her they all began to call:

"Hurrah for our Mamma! She surely can make
The nicest and spiciest Christmas cake!
Hurrah for the Baker! Hurrah for the fun!
Hurrah for our Christmas cake! Now it is done!" ♣

Cookies For Christmas

Spending time together is especially fun for families during the Christmas season. This year, coax the crew into the kitchen for some serious cookie making—and sampling! Mom and Dad can mix the dough, older kids can shape and cut the cookies, and little ones can take charge of the decorating.

Clockwise, from top left, are *Candy Window Sugar Cookies, Meringue Turtledoves, Spritz, Rolled Sugar Cookies, Pizzelles, Pealing Bells, Tiny Holiday Tarts,* and *Scandinavian Almond Bars, Snowmen, Old-Fashioned Sugar Cookies,* and *Swirled Mint Cookies.* Recipes are on pages 136–141.

Rolled Sugar Cookies

2 cups all-purpose flour
1½ teaspoons baking powder
¼ teaspoon salt
⅓ cup butter *or* margarine
⅓ cup shortening
¾ cup sugar
1 egg
1 tablespoon milk
1 teaspoon vanilla
   Creamy Decorative Icing

In a bowl combine flour, baking powder, and salt. In a large mixer bowl beat together butter or margarine and shortening till butter is softened. Add sugar; beat till fluffy. Add egg, milk, and vanilla; beat well. Add flour mixture and beat till well mixed. Divide dough in half. Cover and chill at least 3 hours or till easy to handle.

Roll dough ⅛ inch thick. Cut with cookie cutters. Place on an ungreased cookie sheet. Bake in a 375° oven for 7 to 8 minutes or till done. Remove and cool. If desired, pipe on Creamy Decorative Icing with a decorating bag and decorate with candies. Makes 36 to 48.

Creamy Decorative Icing: In a small mixer bowl beat 1 *egg white*, 2 teaspoons *lemon juice,* and enough sifted *powdered sugar* (1½ to 2 cups) to make icing of piping consistency. If desired, stir in several drops *food coloring.*

Candy Window Cookies: Prepare the dough for Rolled Sugar Cookies as above. Roll out and cut into desired shapes. Place on a foil-lined cookie sheet. Cut out small shapes in the cookie centers. Finely crush 3 ounces *clear hard candy* and spoon enough crushed candy into each center to fill hole. Bake as directed. Peel cookies off foil and cool.

When making candy windows, you'll need to crush the hard candy into fine pieces. Place each color in a small plastic bag and pound it with a rolling pin, the flat edge of a meat mallet, or a hammer. If you decide to use more than one color in a hole, mix the colors as little as possible. As the cookies bake, the candy will melt into "windowpanes."

Scandinavian Almond Bars

1¾ cups all-purpose flour
2 teaspoons baking powder
¼ teaspoon salt
½ cup butter *or* margarine
1 cup sugar
1 egg
½ teaspoon almond extract
   Milk
½ cup sliced almonds, coarsely chopped
   Almond Icing

Stir together flour, baking powder, and salt. In a large mixer bowl beat butter or margarine till softened. Add sugar and beat till fluffy. Add egg and almond extract and beat well. Add flour mixture and beat till well mixed.

Divide dough into fourths. Form each into a 12-inch roll. Place 2 rolls 4 to 5 inches apart on an ungreased cookie sheet. Flatten till 3 inches wide. Repeat with remaining rolls.

Brush flattened rolls with milk and sprinkle with almonds. Bake in a 325° oven for 12 to 14 minutes or till edges are lightly browned. While cookies are still warm, cut crosswise at a diagonal into 1-inch strips. Cool. Drizzle with Almond Icing.

Almond Icing: Stir together 1 cup sifted *powdered sugar,* ¼ teaspoon *almond extract,* and enough *milk* to make icing of drizzling consistency.

Tiny Holiday Tarts

Choose from six different fillings!

- ½ cup butter *or* margarine
- 1 3-ounce package cream cheese, softened
- 1 cup all-purpose flour
  Desired filling

In a small mixer bowl beat together butter or margarine and cream cheese. Stir in flour. Cover and chill about 1 hour or till easy to handle. Shape into 1-inch balls. Press onto bottom and up sides of ungreased 1¾-inch muffin cups. Fill each with *1 rounded teaspoon* filling. Bake in a 325° oven for 25 to 30 minutes or till done. Cool slightly in pan. Remove and cool completely. Makes 24.

Cranberry-Nut Filling: Beat together 1 *egg*, ½ cup packed *brown sugar*, 1 tablespoon melted *butter or margarine*, and 1 teaspoon *vanilla*. Stir in 3 tablespoons chopped *walnuts* and ⅓ cup finely chopped fresh *cranberries*.

Pumpkin Pie Filling: Beat together 1 *egg*, ½ cup canned *pumpkin*, ⅓ cup *sugar*, ¼ cup dairy *sour cream*, 1 tablespoon *milk*, and ½ teaspoon *pumpkin pie spice*. If desired, pipe or dollop *whipped cream* on cooled baked tarts.

Pecan Pie Filling: Beat together 1 *egg*, ¾ cup packed *brown sugar*, 1 tablespoon melted *butter or margarine*, and 1 teaspoon *vanilla*. Stir in ½ cup coarsely chopped *pecans*.

Lemon-Coconut Filling: Beat together 2 *eggs*, ½ cup *sugar*, 2 tablespoons melted *butter or margarine*, ½ teaspoon finely shredded *lemon peel*, and 1 tablespoon *lemon juice*. Stir in ¼ cup flaked *coconut*.

Almond-Raspberry Filling: Divide ¼ cup *red raspberry preserves* among pastries (about ½ teaspoon each). Beat together 1 *egg*, ½ cup *sugar*, and ½ cup *almond paste*, crumbled. Spoon 1 level teaspoon of almond mixture over preserves. Sprinkle with coarsely chopped sliced *almonds*. If desired, drizzle cooled baked tarts with additional *red raspberry preserves*.

Here are some slick storage tricks to help keep holiday happenings running smoothly. To keep crisp cookies snappy and moist cookies soft and chewy, proper storage is a must. Store moist and crisp cookies separately. You can easily restore moisture to soft cookies that have dried out. Just place a wedge of raw apple or a slice of bread underlined with waxed paper into the container and seal tightly. Remove after 24 hours. For long-term storage, you can freeze baked cookies in freezer containers or plastic bags for up to 12 months. Bulk dough, with the exception of meringue type, can be frozen for baking later. Store dough in the freezer for up to 6 months. Thaw before baking.

Pealing Bells

- 2 cups all-purpose flour
- 1½ teaspoons baking powder
- ⅓ cup butter *or* margarine
- ⅓ cup shortening
- ¾ cup sugar
- 1 egg
- 1 tablespoon milk
- 1 teaspoon grated orange peel
- 1 teaspoon vanilla
- 25 maraschino cherries, halved and well drained

Combine flour and baking powder. In a large mixer bowl beat butter or margarine and shortening till butter is softened. Add sugar and beat till fluffy. Add egg, milk, orange peel, and vanilla and beat well. Add flour mixture and beat till well mixed. Cover and chill about 30 minutes or till easy to handle. Shape into two 8-inch rolls. Wrap and chill for several hours or overnight.

Cut into ¼-inch slices. Place cookies on an ungreased cookie sheet. Place a cherry on the bottom of each slice for bell clapper. Fold in sides of slice, overlapping at top and slightly covering cherry. Pinch in sides to resemble bell shape. Bake in a 350° oven for 12 to 14 minutes or till done. Remove and cool. Makes about 64.

Meringue Turtledoves

2 egg whites
½ teaspoon vanilla
¼ teaspoon cream of tartar
½ cup sugar
   Miniature semisweet
   chocolate pieces

Line a large cookie sheet with brown paper or foil. In a small mixer bowl beat egg whites, vanilla, and cream of tartar till soft peaks form. Gradually add sugar, beating till stiff peaks form.

Put egg white mixture in a decorating bag fitted with a ½-inch round tip, filling bag half full. Beginning at head end, squeeze bag gently, moving tip in a clockwise direction to form a question mark with egg white mixture. For lower body, continue squeezing as you move tip about 2½ inches to the right, back left, then right again, releasing pressure as you pull up tip. Repeat with remaining mixture. Place miniature chocolate pieces on head for eye and beak.

Bake in a 300° oven about 15 minutes or till done. Turn off the oven and let cookies dry in the oven with the door closed about 30 minutes. Makes about 24.

Spritz

3½ cups all-purpose flour
1 teaspoon baking powder
1½ cups butter *or* margarine
1 cup sugar
1 egg
1 teaspoon vanilla
½ teaspoon almond extract
   Food coloring (optional)
   Colored sugars *or*
      decorative candies
      (optional)

Stir together flour and baking powder. In a large mixer bowl beat butter or margarine till softened. Add sugar and beat till fluffy. Add egg, vanilla, and almond extract and beat well. Gradually add flour mixture and beat till well mixed. To ensure easy passage through the cookie press, do not chill dough.

If desired, tint dough with food coloring. Force dough through a cookie press onto an ungreased cookie sheet. Decorate with colored sugars or candies, if desired. Bake in a 400° oven for 7 to 8 minutes or till done. Remove and cool. Makes about 60.

Pizzelles

2 cups all-purpose flour
1 tablespoon baking powder
1½ teaspoons ground nutmeg
½ teaspoon ground
      cardamom
3 eggs
¾ cup sugar
⅓ cup butter *or* margarine,
      melted and cooled
2 teaspoons vanilla

Stir together flour, baking powder, nutmeg, and cardamom. In a small mixer bowl beat eggs with an electric mixer on high speed about 4 minutes or till thick and lemon colored. With mixer on medium speed, gradually beat in sugar. Beat in cooled, melted butter or margarine and vanilla. Add flour mixture; beat on low speed till combined.

Heat a pizzelle iron on rangetop over medium heat (or heat an electric pizzelle iron according to manufacturer's directions) till a drop of water sizzles on the grid. Reduce the heat to medium-low. Place a slightly rounded tablespoon of batter in the center of the round grid. Squeeze lid to close. (Or, use an electric pizzelle iron according to manufacturer's directions.) Turn wafer out onto a paper towel to cool. Repeat with remaining batter. Makes 18.

Wishing Cookies

3¼ cups all-purpose flour
  1 teaspoon baking soda
  1 teaspoon ground cinnamon
  ¾ teaspoon ground ginger
  ¼ teaspoon ground nutmeg
  1 cup butter *or* margarine
1½ cups sugar
  1 egg
  2 tablespoons molasses
  1 tablespoon water
  ½ teaspoon grated orange *or* lemon peel
  Lace Icing

Stir together flour, baking soda, cinnamon, ginger, and nutmeg. In a large mixer bowl beat together butter or margarine till softened, Add sugar and beat till fluffy. Add egg, molasses, water, and peel and beat well. Gradually add flour mixture and beat till well mixed. Cover and chill about 2 hours or till easy to handle. Roll dough ⅛ inch thick. Cut with cookie cutters. Place on an ungreased cookie sheet. Bake in a 375° oven about 8 minutes or till done. Remove and cool. With a decorating bag and writing tip, pipe on a design with Lace Icing. Makes about 100.

Lace Icing: Stir together 2 cups sifted *powdered sugar*, ½ teaspoon *vanilla*, and enough *light cream or milk* (about 2 tablespoons) to make icing of piping consistency. If desired, tint with a few drops *food coloring*.

Place a cookie in the palm of your hand. Press in the center with one finger. If the cookie breaks into three pieces and you can eat all three without saying a word, you get to make a wish. (Keeping quiet is the hard part!)

Swirled Mint Cookies

2 cups all-purpose flour
½ teaspoon baking powder
1 cup butter *or* margarine
1 cup sugar
1 egg
1 teaspoon vanilla
½ teaspoon peppermint extract
10 drops red food coloring
10 drops green food coloring

Combine flour and baking powder. In a large mixer bowl beat butter or margarine till softened. Add sugar and beat till fluffy. Add egg, vanilla, and peppermint extract and beat well. Add flour mixture and beat till well mixed. Divide into thirds. Stir red food coloring into one third, stir green food coloring into another, and leave remaining third plain. Cover each and chill about 1 hour or till easy to handle.

Divide each color of dough into 4 parts. On a lightly floured surface roll each into a ½-inch-diameter rope. Place 1 red, 1 green, and 1 plain rope side by side. Twist together. Slice into ½-inch pieces for larger cookies or ¼-inch pieces for smaller ones. Carefully roll into balls, blending colors as little as possible. Place about 2 inches apart on an ungreased cookie sheet.

Flatten to ¼-inch thickness with the bottom of a glass dipped in additional sugar. Repeat with remaining dough. Bake in a 375° oven till done (allow 8 to 10 minutes for larger cookies or 6 to 8 minutes for smaller ones). Remove; cool. Makes about 72 (2½-inch) or 144 (1¼-inch) cookies.

Using a rope of each color, twist three ropes together to swirl the colors. Cut the twisted ropes into ½-inch or ¼-inch pieces, depending on how big you like your cookies. Then, shape each piece into a ball. Be careful not to mix the colors too much, so you can see all three colors. Place balls on a cookie sheet. Using the bottom of a glass dipped in sugar, flatten the cookies to ¼-inch thickness.

Old-Fashioned Sugar Cookies

4½ cups all-purpose flour
2 teaspoons baking powder
1 teaspoon baking soda
½ teaspoon salt
½ teaspoon ground nutmeg
1¼ cups shortening
2 cups sugar
2 eggs
1 teaspoon vanilla
½ teaspoon lemon extract
1 cup buttermilk *or* sour milk*

In a mixing bowl stir together flour, baking powder, baking soda, salt, and nutmeg. In a large mixer bowl beat shortening for 30 seconds. Add sugar and beat till fluffy. Add eggs, vanilla, and lemon extract and beat well. Add flour mixture and buttermilk alternately to shortening mixture, beating till well mixed. Divide in half. Cover and chill for at least 3 hours or till easy to handle.

For large cookies, roll dough ½ inch thick. Cut into rounds with a 3-inch cookie cutter. For small cookies, roll dough ⅜ inch thick and cut into rounds with a 2-inch cutter. Place cookies 2½ inches apart on an ungreased cookie sheet. Sprinkle cookies with additional sugar. Bake in a 375° oven for 10 to 12 minutes or till done. Remove and cool. Makes 24 large or 48 small cookies.

*Note: For sour milk, combine 1 tablespoon *lemon juice or vinegar* and enough *milk* to make 1 cup. Let stand for 5 minutes.

Snowmen

1 cup butter *or* margarine
½ cup sugar
1 teaspoon vanilla
2¼ cups all-purpose flour
   Miniature semisweet
     chocolate pieces
   Powdered Sugar Icing
     (see page 38)
   Thin ribbon
   Large gumdrops
   Powdered sugar

In a mixer bowl beat butter or margarine till softened. Add sugar and beat till fluffy. Beat in vanilla. Add flour; beat till mixed. For each snowman, shape dough into 3 balls: one 1-inch, one ¾-inch, and one ½-inch ball. Place balls on an ungreased cookie sheet in decreasing sizes with sides touching. Press together slightly. Insert 2 chocolate pieces in smallest ball for eyes, then 1 in middle ball and 2 in largest ball for buttons. Bake in a 325° oven for 18 to 20 minutes or till done. Carefully remove and cool.

Tie a 6-inch piece of ribbon around the neck of each snowman. For each hat, sprinkle sugar on a cutting board. Place 1 gumdrop on board and sprinkle with more sugar. Roll gumdrop into an oval about ⅛ inch thick. Curve to form a cone and press together to seal. Attach to head with icing. Lightly sprinkle snowmen with powdered sugar. If broom is desired, tint remaining icing with food coloring; pipe onto cookies. Makes about 24.

New Zealand Holly Cookies

2 cups all-purpose flour
1 cup sugar
1 teaspoon ground cinnamon
¾ teaspoon baking powder
¼ teaspoon salt
½ cup butter *or* margarine
1 slightly beaten egg
¼ cup milk
⅔ cup raspberry jam
2 cups sifted powdered sugar
½ teaspoon vanilla
2 to 3 tablespoons milk
   Red cinnamon candies
   Green food coloring

In a medium mixing bowl combine flour, sugar, cinnamon, baking powder, and salt. Cut in butter or margarine till pieces are the size of small peas. Make a well in the center. Combine egg and ¼ cup milk; add all at once to dry mixture. Stir till moistened. On a lightly floured surface roll dough to ⅛-inch thickness. Cut into 2-inch circles or into flowers with a cookie cutter. Place on an ungreased cookie sheet. Bake in a 375° oven for 8 to 10 minutes or till light brown on the bottom. Cool on a wire rack. Place about ½ teaspoon raspberry jam on the bottom of 1 round; top with another round. Repeat with remaining cookies.

In a small mixing bowl stir together powdered sugar, vanilla, and enough milk to make of glazing consistency. Spread top of each cookie with some of the glaze. For holly berries, while icing is still wet, drop 2 or 3 cinnamon candies on each cookie. Let icing dry. Using a small paintbrush, paint several holly leaves and a stem on each cookie with green food coloring. Makes 54.

The Year We Had A 'Sensible' Christmas

—Henry Appers

For as long as I could remember our family had talked about a sensible Christmas. Every year, my mother would limp home from shopping or she would sit beside the kitchen table after hours of baking, close her eyes, catch her breath and say, "This is the last time I'm going to exhaust myself with all this holiday fuss. Next year we're going to have a *sensible* Christmas."

And always my father, if he was within earshot, would agree. "It's not worth the time and expense."

While we were kids, my sister and I lived in dread that Mom and Dad would go through with their rash vows of a reduced Christmas. But if they ever *did,* we reasoned, there were several things about Christmas that we, ourselves, would like to amend. And two of these were, namely, my mother's Uncle Lloyd and his wife, Aunt Amelia.

Many a time Lizzie and I wondered why families had to have relatives, and especially why it was our fate to inherit Uncle Lloyd and Aunt Amelia. They were a sour and a formal pair who came to us every Christmas, bringing Lizzie and me handkerchiefs as gifts and expecting in return silence, respect, service and for me to surrender my bedroom.

Lizzie and I had understood early that Great-uncle Lloyd was, indeed, a poor man, and we were sympathetic to this. But we dared to think that even poverty provided no permit for them to be stiff and unwarm and a nuisance in the bargain. Still we accepted Great-uncle Lloyd and Great-aunt Amelia as our lot and they were, for years, as much the tradition of Christmas as mistletoe.

Then came my first year in college. It must have been some perverse reaction to my being away, but Mom started it. *This* was to be the year of the sensible Christmas. "By not exhausting ourselves with all the folderol," she wrote me, "we'll at last have the energy and the time to appreciate Christmas."

Dad, as usual, went along with Mom, but added his own touch. We were not to spend more than a dollar for each of our gifts to one another. "For once," Dad said, "we'll worry about the thought behind the gift, and not about its price."

It was I who suggested that our sensible Christmas be limited to the immediate family, just the four of us. The motion was carried. Mom wrote a gracious letter to Great-uncle Lloyd explaining that what with my being away in school and for one reason and another we

weren't going to do much about Christmas, so maybe they would enjoy it more if they didn't make their usual great effort to come. Dad enclosed a check, an unexpected boon.

I arrived home from college that Christmas wondering what to expect. A wreath on the front door provided a fitting nod to the season. There was a Christmas tree in the living room and I must admit that, af first, it made my heart twinge. Artificial, the tree was small and seemed without character when compared to the luxurious, forest-smelling firs of former years. But the more I looked at it, with our brightly wrapped dollar gifts under it, the friendlier it became and I began to think of the mess of real trees, and their fire threat, and how ridiculous, how really unnatural it was to bring a living tree inside a house anyway. Already the idea of a sensible Christmas was getting to me.

Christmas Eve Mom cooked a good but simple dinner and afterward we all sat together in the living room. "This is nice," Lizzie purred, a-snuggle in the big cabbage rose chair.

"Yes," Dad agreed. "It's quiet. I'm not tired out. For once, I think I can stay awake until church."

"If this were last Christmas," I reminded Mom, "you'd still be in the kitchen with your hours of 'last-minute' jobs. More cookies. More fruit cake." I recalled the compulsive way I used to nibble at Mom's fruit cake. "But I never really liked it," I confessed with a laugh.

"I didn't know that," Mom said. She was thoughtful for a moment. Then her face brightened. "But Aunt Amelia—how *she* adored it!"

"Maybe she was just being nice," Lizzie said undiplomatically.

Then we fell silent. Gradually we took to reading. Dad did slip off into a short snooze before church.

Christmas morning we slept late, and once up we breakfasted before advancing to our gifts. And what a time we had with those! We laughed merrily at our own originality and cleverness. I gave Mom a cluster-pin that I had fashioned out of aluminum measuring spoons and had adorned with rhinestones. Mother wore the pin all day or, at least, until we went out to Dempsey's.

At Dempsey's, the best restaurant in town, we had a wonderful, unrushed feast. There was only one awkward moment just after the consomme
continued

was served. We started to lift our spoons. Then Dad suggested that we say grace and we all started to hold hands around the table as we always do at home, and then we hesitated and drew our hand back, and then in unison we refused to be intimidated by a public eating place and held hands and said grace.

Nothing much happened the rest of the day. In the evening I wandered into the kitchen, opened the refrigerator, poked around for a minute, closed the door and came back to the living room.

"That's a joke," I reported, with no idea at all of the effect my next remark would have. "I went to pick at the turkey."

In tones that had no color, Mother spoke. "I knew that's what you went out there for. I've been waiting for it to happen."

No longer could she stay the sobs that now burst forth from her. "Kate!" Dad cried, rushing to her.

"Forgive me. Forgive me," Mom kept muttering.

"For what, dear? Please tell us."

"For this terrible, dreadful, sensible Christmas."

Each of us knew what she meant. Our Christmas had been as artificial as that Christmas tree; at some point the spirit of the day had just quietly crept away from us. In our efforts at common sense we had lost the reason for Christmas and had forgotten about others; this denied Him whose birthday it was all about. Each of us, we knew full well, had contributed to this selfishness, but Mom was taking the blame.

As her sobs became sniffles and our assurances began to take effect, Mom addressed us more coherently, in Mom's own special incoherent way. "I should have been in the kitchen last night instead of wasting my time," she began, covering up her sentimentality with anger. "So you don't like my fruit cake, Harry? Too bad. Aunt Amelia *really* adores it! And Elizabeth, even if she doesn't, you shouldn't be disrespectful to the old soul. Do you know who else loves my fruit cake? Mrs. Donegan down the street loves it. And she didn't get her gift from me this year. Why? Because we're being *sensible*." Then

Mom turned on Dad, wagging her finger at him. "We can't afford to save on Christmas, Lewis! It shuts off the heart."

That seemed to sum it up.

Yet, Lizzie had another way of saying it. She put it in a letter to me at school, a letter as lovely as Lizzie herself. "Mom feels," Lizzie wrote, "that the strains and stresses are the birth pangs of Christmas. So do I. I'm certain that it is out of our efforts and tirednesss and turmoil that some sudden, quiet, shining, priceless thing occurs each year and if all we produce is only a feeling as long as a flicker, it is worth the bother."

Just as my family came to call that The Christmas That Never Was, the next one became the Prodigal Christmas. It was the most festive, and the most frazzling time in our family's history— not because we spent any more money, but because we threw all of ourselves into the joy of Christmas. In the woods at the edge of town we cut the largest tree we'd ever had. Lizzie and I swathed the house in greens. Delicious smells came from the kitchen as Mom baked and baked and baked . . . . We laughed and sang carols and joked. Even that dour pair, Great-uncle Lloyd and Great-aunt Amelia were almost, but not quite gay. Still, it was through them that I felt that quick surge of warmth, that glorious "feeling as long as a flicker," that made Christmas meaningful.

We had just sat down in our own dining room and had reached out our hands to one another for our circle of grace. When I took Great-aunt Amelia's hand in mine, it happened. I learned something about her and giving that, without this Christmas, I might never have known.

The hand that I held was cold. I became aware of how gnarled her fingers were, how years of agonizing arthritis had twisted them. Only then did I think of the handkerchiefs that Lizzie and I had received this year, as in all the years before. For the first time I saw clearly the delicate embroidery, the painstaking needlework— Great-aunt Amelia's yearly gift of love to, and for, us. ♣

Christmas Cards

Cards Sent _____

_____
_____
_____
_____
_____
_____
_____
_____
_____

Cards Received _____

_____
_____
_____
_____
_____
_____
_____
_____
_____
_____
_____

Kids' Holiday Artwork

Christmas Gifts

Gifts Given

Gifts Received

_____

_____

_____

_____

_____

_____

_____

_____

_____

_____

_____

_____

_____

_____

_____

_____

_____

_____

_____

_____

_____

_____

_____

_____

_____

_____

_____

How We Spent the Holidays

Christmas Eve

Where We Celebrated _____

How We Celebrated _____

_____
_____
_____
_____
_____
_____
_____
_____
_____
_____
_____
_____
_____
_____
_____
_____
_____
_____
_____
_____
_____
_____
_____
_____
_____
_____

Christmas Day

Where We Celebrated _____

How We Celebrated _____

_____

_____

_____

_____

_____

_____

_____

_____

_____

_____

_____

_____

_____

_____

_____

_____

_____

_____

_____

_____

_____

_____

_____

_____

Special Moments to Treasure

Photos and other holiday memorabilia

SHARING
THE
SPIRIT

At Christmas be merry,
and thankful withal,
And feast thy poor neighbors,
the great with the small.

—*Thomas Tusser*

Tilly's Christmas

—Louisa M. Alcott

"I'm so glad tomorrow is Christmas, because I'm going to have lots of presents."

"So am I glad, though I don't expect any presents but a pair of mittens."

"And so am I, but I shan't have any presents at all."

As the three little girls trudged home from school they said these things, and as Tilly spoke, both the others looked at her with pity and some surprise, for she spoke cheerfully, and they wondered how she could be happy when she was so poor she could have no presents on Christmas.

"Don't you wish you could find a purse full of money right here in the path?" said Kate, the child who was going to have "lots of presents."

"Oh, don't I, if I could keep it honestly!" and Tilly's eyes shone at the thought.

"What would you buy?" asked Bessy, rubbing her cold hands, and longing for her mittens.

"I'd buy a pair of large warm blankets, a load of wood, a shawl for mother, and a pair of shoes for me; and if there was enough left, I'd buy Bessy a new hat, and then she needn't wear Ben's old felt one," answered Tilly.

The girls laughed at that; but Bessy pulled the funny hat over her ears, and said she was much obliged, but she'd rather have candy.

"Let's look and maybe we *can* find a purse. People are always going about with money at Christmas time, and someone may lose it here," said Kate.

So, as they went along the snowy road, they looked about them, half in earnest, half in fun. Suddenly Tilly sprang forward exclaiming:

"I see it! I've found it!"

The others followed, but all stopped disappointed; for it wasn't a purse, it was only a little bird. It lay upon the snow with its wings spread and feebly fluttering, as if too weak to fly. Its little feet were benumbed with cold; its once bright eyes were dull with pain, and instead of a blithe song, it could only utter a faint chirp, now and then, as if crying for help.

"Nothing but a stupid old robin; how provoking!" cried Kate, sitting down to rest.

"I shan't touch it. I found one once, and took care of it, and the ungrateful thing flew away the minute it was well," said Bessy, creeping under Kate's shawl, and putting her hands under her chin to warm them.

"Poor little birdie! How pitiful he looks, and how glad he must be to see some one coming to help him! I'll take him up gently, and carry him home to Mother. Don't be frightened, dear, I'm your friend"; and Tilly knelt down in the snow, stretching her hand to the bird with the tenderest pity in her face.

Kate and Bessy laughed.

"Don't stop for that thing; it's getting late and cold; let's go on and look for the purse," they said, moving away.

"You wouldn't leave it to die!" cried Tilly. "I'd rather have the bird than the money, so I shan't look any more. The purse wouldn't be mine, and I should only be tempted to keep it; but this poor thing will thank and love me, and I'm *so* glad I came in time."

Gently lifting the bird, Tilly felt its tiny cold claws cling to her hand, and saw its dim eyes brighten as it nestled down with a grateful chirp.

"Now I've got a Christmas present after all," she said, smiling, as they walked on. "I always wanted a bird, and this one will be such a pretty pet for me."

"He'll fly away the first chance he gets, and die anyhow; so you'd better not waste your time over him," said Bessy.

"He can't pay you for taking care of him, and my mother says it isn't worth while to help folks that can't help us," added Kate.

continued

"My mother says, 'Do as you'd be done by'; and I'm sure I'd like any one to help me if I was dying of cold and hunger. 'Love your neighbor as yourself,' is another of her sayings. This bird is my little neighbor, and I'll love and care for him, as I often wish our rich neighbor would love and care for us," answered Tilly, breathing her warm breath over the benumbed bird, who looked up at her with confiding eyes, quick to feel and know a friend.

"What a funny girl you are," said Kate, "caring for that silly bird, and talking about loving your neighbor in that sober way. Mr. King don't care a bit for you, and never will, though he knows how poor you are; so I don't think your plan amounts to much."

"I believe it, though; and shall do my part, anyway. Good night. I hope you'll have a merry Christmas, and lots of pretty things," answered Tilly, as they parted.

Her eyes were full, and she felt *so* poor as she went on alone toward the little old house where she lived. It would have been so pleasant to know that she was going to have some of the pretty things all children love to find in their full stockings on Christmas morning. And pleasanter still to have been able to give her mother something nice. So many comforts were needed, and there was no hope of getting them; for they could barely get food and fire.

"Never mind, birdie, we'll make the best of what we have, and be merry in spite of everything. *You* shall have a happy Christmas, anyway; and I know God won't forget us, if everyone else does."

She stopped a minute to wipe her eyes, and lean her cheek against the bird's soft breast, finding great comfort in the little creature, though it could only love her, nothing more.

"See, Mother, what a nice present I've found," she cried, going in with a cheery face that was like sunshine in the dark room.

"I'm glad of that, dearie; for I haven't been able to get my little girl anything but a rosy apple. Poor bird! Give it some of your warm bread and milk."

"Why, Mother, what a big bowlful! I'm afraid you gave me all the milk," said Tilly, smiling over the nice, steaming supper that stood ready for her.

"I've had plenty, dear. Sit down and dry your wet feet, and put the bird in my basket on this warm flannel."

Tilly peeped into the closet and saw nothing there but dry bread.

"Mother's given me all the milk, and is going without her tea, 'cause she knows I'm hungry. Now I'll surprise her, and she shall have a good supper too. She is going to split wood, and I'll fix it while she's gone."

So Tilly put down the old teapot, carefully poured out a part of her milk, and from her pocket produced a great, plummy bun, that one of the school children had given her, and she had saved for her mother. A slice of the dry bread was nicely toasted, and the bit of butter set by for her to put on it. When the mother came in there was the table drawn up in a warm place, a hot cup of tea ready, and Tilly and birdie waiting for her.

Such a poor little supper, and yet such a happy one; for love, charity, and contentment were guests there, and that Christmas Eve was a blither one than that up at the great house, where lights shone, fires blazed, and a great tree glittered, and music sounded, as the children danced and played.

"We must go to bed early, for we've only wood enough to last over tomorrow. I shall be paid for my work the day after, and then we can get some," said Tilly's mother, as they sat by the fire.

"If my bird was only a fairy bird, and would give us three wishes, how nice it would be! Poor dear, he can't give me anything; but it's no matter," answered Tilly, looking at the robin, who lay in the basket with his head under his wing, a mere feathery bunch.

"He can give you one thing, Tilly,—the pleasure of doing good. That is one of the sweetest things of life; and the poor can enjoy it as well as the rich."

Tilly went, taking her bird to sleep in his basket near by, lest he should be lonely in the night.

When Tilly opened the door next morning, she gave a loud cry, clapped her hands, and then stood still, quite speechless with wonder and delight. There, before the door, lay a great pile of wood, all ready to burn, a big bundle and a basket, with a lovely nosegay of winter roses, holly, and evergreen tied to the handle.

"Oh, Mother, did the fairies do it?" cried Tilly, pale with her happiness, as she seized the basket, while her mother took in the bundle.

"Yes, dear, the best and dearest fairy in the world, called 'Charity.' She walks abroad at Christmas time, does beautiful deeds like this, and does not stay to be thanked," answered her mother with full eyes, as she undid the parcel.

There they were—the warm, thick blankets, the comfortable shawl, the new shoes, and, best of all, a pretty winter hat for Bessy. The basket was full of good things to eat, and on the flowers lay a paper saying:

"For the little girl who loves her neighbor as herself."

"Mother, I really think my bird is a fairy bird, and all these splendid things come from him," said Tilly, laughing and crying with joy.

It really did seem so, for, as she spoke, the robin flew to the table, hopped to the nosegay, and, perching among the roses, began to chirp with all his little might. The sun streamed in on the flowers, bird, and happy child, and no one saw a shadow glide away from the window; no one ever knew that Mr. King had seen and heard the little girls the night before, or dreamed that the rich neighbor had learned a lesson from the poor neighbor.

And Tilly's bird *was* a fairy bird; for, by her love and tenderness to the helpless thing, she brought good gifts to herself, happiness to the unknown giver of them, and a faithful little friend who did not fly away, but stayed with her till the snow was gone, making summer for her in the wintertime. ♣

As her mother spoke, with her tired hand softly stroking her little daughter's hair, Tilly suddenly started and pointed to the window, saying, in a frightened whisper:

"I saw a face,—a man's face, looking in! It's gone now, but I truly saw it."

"Some traveler attracted by the light perhaps. I'll go and see." And Tilly's mother went to the door.

No one was there. The wind blew cold, the stars shone, the snow lay white on field and wood, and the Christmas moon was glittering in the sky.

"What sort of face was it?" asked Tilly's mother, coming back.

"A pleasant sort of face, I think; but I was so startled I don't quite know what it was like. I wish we had a curtain there," said Tilly.

"I like to have our light shine out in the evening, for the road is dark and lonely just here, and the twinkle of our lamp is pleasant to people's eyes as they go by. We can do so little for our neighbors, I am glad to cheer the way for them. Now put these poor old shoes to dry, and go to bed, dearie; I'll come soon.

Cheery Cherry Designs

Stenciling is a simple way to make holiday table settings for your home, bazaars, or gifts— especially when you craft a merry, cherry Christmas using our luscious design.

MATERIALS

For napkin ties (set of four)
Eight 1-inch-diameter red beads
8 small artificial leaves; glue
1⅔ yards of ⅛-inch-diameter green cording
For place mats and napkins (set of four)
½ yard of heavy white cotton duck fabric (place mats)
½ yard of white poly-cotton fabric (napkins)
Red sewing thread
Waxed stencil paper
Piece of glass
Stencil brushes and knife
Red and green fabric paint

INSTRUCTIONS

NAPKIN TIES: Cut the cord into four equal lengths. Slip one length of cord through one bead; knot the end of the cord. Pull knot through the hole and glue to bead. Repeat with another bead to complete the cord. Follow the same procedure to make four ties.

Glue one leaf to top of each bead. Trim leaf if necessary. Tie finished tie around a napkin.

PLACE MATS: Trace the full-size pattern, page 167, onto tissue paper. Flop the pattern to complete it. Cut out four 13x17½-inch place mats from duck.

Run a row of tiny stay stitches ¼ inch from the edge (dotted line on pattern). Pull out all the horizontal threads up to the stay stitching to make fringe. Trim the fringe evenly. With red thread, run a row of stitching around the edge slightly above the fringed edge. Remove the stay stitching.

To do the stenciling, cut three 3x5-inch pieces of stencil paper. Draw the pattern for the leaves on one paper. Draw the cherries on another and the stems and veins on the third. Stack the three stencil papers together to see if the parts line up properly. Make register marks on the cherry and stem-and-vein stencils by outlining the leaves with a broken line.

Place the stencil papers, one at a time, on a piece of glass. Using a stencil knife, cut out the designs.

Stencil cherry clusters in each corner; stencil leaves only on each side between clusters.

Tape the fabric to a smooth board; tape the stencil in place. Dip the tip of the brush lightly into paint. Brush off the excess paint onto a scrap. Brush the paint through the cut stencil from the edge to the center (practice on scrap fabric first). Add more paint to the brush as necessary.

Stencil the leaves first, then the cherries, and finally the stems and veins. Mix a little red with the green paint to arrive at a dark green for the stems and veins.

Iron the wrong side of the place mat to set the paint after it is dry.

NAPKINS: Cut four 16-inch squares from poly-cotton fabric.

Run a row of stay stitches ¼ inch from the edges. Finish the edges as for the place mats. Use the leaf pattern to stencil around the edge of the napkin.

Elegant Cross-Stitch Tablecloth

Share your stitchery talents with holiday guests by making this festive holiday linen. The elegant fabric, with its holly, wreath, and tree motifs, is designed especially for counted embroidery.

MATERIALS

43x57-inch piece of Zweigart® Alba fabric (available through Art Needlework Treasure Trove, Box 2440, Grand Central Station, New York, NY 10163)
No. 5 pearl cotton floss in colors listed under the color key
Embroidery hoop and needle
Graph paper
Felt-tip pens

INSTRUCTIONS

To prepare the patterns, chart the diagrams, *opposite,* onto graph paper, using felt-tip marking pens. Make a mirror image by flopping the symbols to complete the two patterns.

To stitch the tablecloth, work each stitch over one thread of fabric, using pearl cotton floss.

Find the center point of each fabric square to begin stitching. Alternately stitch a wreath and tree in each square.

Continue alternating the motifs to fill the length and width of the tablecloth. Trim the woven borders with single holly motifs, if desired (see photograph).

To finish the tablecloth, hem the raw edges of the cloth, or border the edges with a decorative trim.

To use the patterns in other ways, consider cross-stitching the wreath and tree motifs down the center of a fabric strip to make a table runner. Or work designs over one thread of hardanger for festive coasters.

Use the tree and wreath motifs, minus the holly borders, and work them over one thread of fabric for delicate ornaments. Cut out the shapes and sew them to a fabric backing, leaving an opening for turning. Stuff with fiberfill and stitch the opening closed. Attach a ribbon loop for hanging. Sew colored beads and pearls onto ornaments for highlights, if desired.

You can use the motifs to stitch a Christmas coverlet, too. Work each design on hardanger fabric; alternate a cross-stitched square with a plain fabric square. Sew squares together; bind with sashing strips, and quilt with Christmas motifs or other traditional quilting patterns.

With just a little imagination, it's easy to create pillows, sweet-scented sachets, box-top covers, and a variety of other Christmas projects.

Cross-stitch tips
Although the back of a stitchery may not seem important, many embroiderers care about the uniformity of the stitches on the underside of their work. To make the wrong side of your tablecloth as attractive as possible, follow these suggestions.

Whenever possible, stitch so the direction of the threads on the reverse side of the tablecloth is vertical. Accomplish this by working across a row, stitching half of the crosses. Then, reverse the stitching to complete the cross-stitched row.

When stitching with a variety of colors, you need not end your thread every time you complete a small color area. Carry the thread across the back of the fabric by slipping the threaded needle under the previously stitched crosses to the point where embroidery begins again with that color.

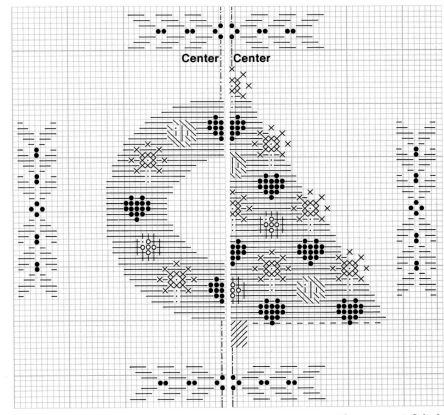

1 Square = 1 Stitch

COLOR KEY

⊟ Green	⊞ Purple	◩ Brown
◉ Red	◲ Blue	⊡ Light Blue
⊠ Yellow	⊡ Gray	◪ Light Purple

Patchwork Table Runner

If you love the country look or know someone who does, you'll enjoy every stitch in this bright-colored sampler. Use the patterns shown or your own favorites, then combine prints, solids, and calicoes to make this cheerful table covering.

Finished size is approximately 17x69 inches.

MATERIALS
1¾ yards of white fabric (1 yard for backing)
⅝ yard of three different red prints
⅝ yard of two different green prints
⅜ yard of red and green print on white background
¼ yard each of red and green solid-color fabrics
1 yard of lightweight quilt batting
Sewing and quilting threads
Embroidery floss
Graph paper

INSTRUCTIONS
Note: Preshrink all fabrics. Use ¼-inch seams throughout.

For the quilt squares
Draw 12-inch squares on graph paper. Draw in lines for each pattern as directed on page 166. For each pattern piece, cut a template, adding a ¼-inch seam allowance all around.

WATER WHEEL: Refer to the drawing, page 166. On graph paper, draw a 2-inch square (6 and 2) and a 4-inch square. Cut the 4-inch square in half diagonally for triangle pattern (7 and 9), adding

seam allowances to each piece. Cut out templates.

Cut pieces from fabrics as indicated on diagram, page 166.

Stitch triangles 7 and 9 together to form larger squares. Stitch squares 6 and 2 together to form larger squares. Arrange squares as indicated. Stitch squares into rows; stitch rows into blocks.

BIRD: Enlarge pattern, page 166; make templates for heart, leaf, bird, and wing. Cut patterns from fabrics, referring to photograph for colors. Cut a 12½-inch white square and position pattern pieces as shown in the diagram. Hand-appliqué pieces into place. Embroider stems and bird's eye.

LOG CABIN FOUR-PATCH: Refer to diagram, page 166, and cut four 2½-inch red squares for centers. Cut 1½-inch strips of white (2), green print (7), and red print (4). *Note:* A ¼-inch seam allowance is included in these measurements. Piece each square as shown in diagram. Stitch squares together to form block.

VARIABLE STAR: Refer to pattern, page 166, and draw two 4-inch squares onto graph paper. Draw an X on one square, dividing it into four triangles; cut apart and use one triangle for pattern piece. Add seams; cut templates.

continued

Cut pieces from fabrics as indicated in drawing and color key, *below, right.* Stitch triangles 3, 5, and 9 together to form squares. Refer to drawing for assembly.

BEAR PAW: See pattern, *below, right,* and make the following templates: a 3½-inch square, two 1¾-inch squares, a ½-inch square, and a 1½x5-inch rectangle. Cut a 1¾-inch square in half diagonally for triangle pattern. Add seams; cut pieces from fabrics. Sew triangles 5 and 9 together to form squares. Refer to drawing for assembly.

Assembly

Align the pieced squares side by side as desired. From solid-color green fabric, cut four 1½x12½-inch sashing strips, two 1½x14-inch end border strips, and four 1½x64½-inch side border strips. From white print, cut two 1x14½-inch strips and two 1x67½-inch strips. *Note:* Long strips will have to be pieced.

Sew a green sashing strip between each of the finished quilt blocks. Stitch a green side border strip to each long edge of the panel. Stitch the green end border strips to the ends of the panel. Sew

white print border strips to the green strips.

Cut batting to measure 14x66 inches. Cut and piece the backing from white fabric to measure 18x70 inches. Center and layer the three pieces; baste together and quilt as desired (don't quilt borders). Trim backing to size of pieced top. Press under raw edge of backing ¼ inch. Set aside.

For prairie-point edging

Draw a 2½-inch square for the master pattern. Cut a total of 96 squares from three red prints (32

of each fabric). Fold squares in half diagonally, then in half diagonally again, and press. *Note:* Raw edge of fabric should measure 2½ inches. Lay out runner panel right side up. Place points along edge of panel, with raw edges aligned (pointing away from edge).

Alternate the prints; use eight points along each short side and 40 points along each long side. Sew through the pieced top border only, ¼ inch from the edge. Turn under seam allowances of points and top; press. Slip-stitch backing to wrong side of points.

BIRD

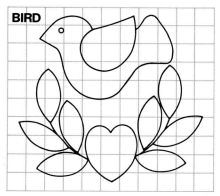

1 Square = 1 Inch

LOG CABIN FOUR-PATCH

VARIABLE STAR

BEAR'S PAW

WATER WHEEL

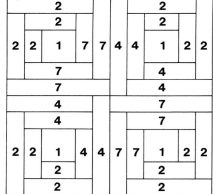

COLOR KEY

1. Red	4. Red Print	7. Green Print
2. White	5. Red Dot	8. Green Print
3. Green	6. Red Print	9. White Print

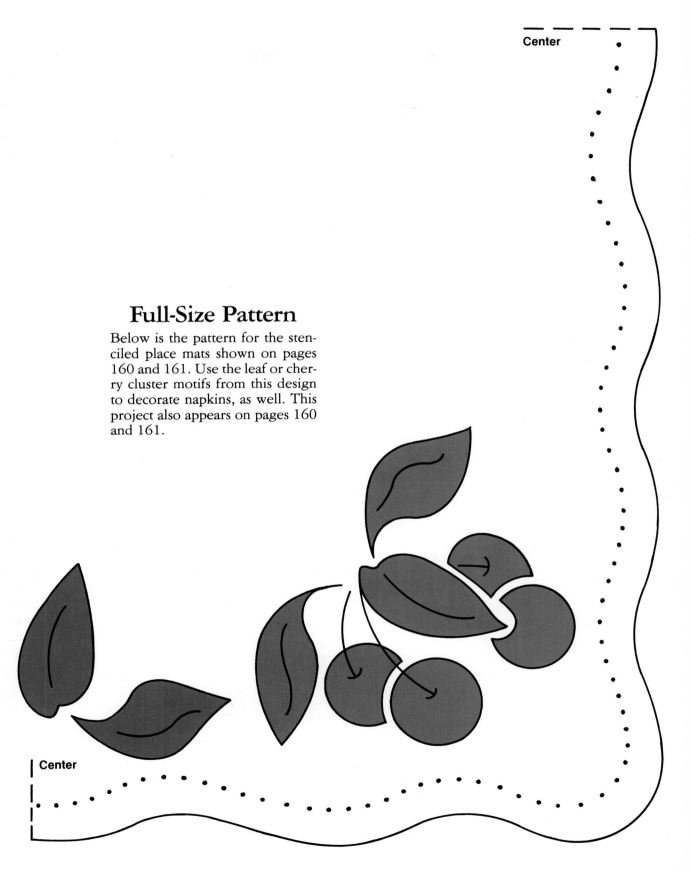

Center

Full-Size Pattern

Below is the pattern for the stenciled place mats shown on pages 160 and 161. Use the leaf or cherry cluster motifs from this design to decorate napkins, as well. This project also appears on pages 160 and 161.

Center

The Rileys' Christmas Tree

—Eliza Orne White

The day before Christmas, something very pleasant happened: Priscilla and her mother came to make the Bensons a long visit.

When Molly saw her dear cousin once more, she flung her arms around her, and hugged and kissed her as if she could never leave off.

"You have got on a pretty blue dress," Priscilla observed, looking at her critically, "and you are taller, but I shall love you just the same."

"I must show you Nonesuch," Molly said, running to find her favorite. She picked her up and held out her right front paw, that Priscilla might shake hands with her.

"This is your cousin Priscilla, Nonesuch," she said gravely.

Priscilla and Nonesuch shook hands, and became fast friends at once.

Priscilla was then shown all Molly's dolls. She thought that George Washington had rather a conceited look, but she supposed it was natural, as he was the only brother among so many sisters. This made Molly very unhappy, but she was pleased to have Priscilla take a great fancy to Jane. She said she put one at ease. She was rather in awe of the Princess and Sylvia.

Later, at dinner, she was very much afraid of Molly's aunt Mary and of her papa, and of Turner and Flora; but she liked Ruth, because, as she expressed it, she was a "grown-up Molly."

After dinner, Julia came over, and although Priscilla did not have a word to say to her at first, the three little girls grew very sociable before many minutes passed.

"Something nice is going to happen this afternoon," Molly confided to Priscilla. "Miss Sylvia is going with Flora, and Julia, and me, to take some Christmas presents to Patrick's children."

"He is the man who makes our fires," Julia explained.

"We went to his house," Molly proceeded, "to take Priscilla the Second."

"That's the kitten."

"She knows it's the kitten, Julia. They didn't seem to have anything to play with (not that it matters much, for one can always pretend); so Aunt Mary suggested that we should dress some dolls for them. She and Miss Sylvia and Ruth dressed them mostly, but we children helped, and we sewed up some muslin bags this morning in school, and filled them with candy. Turner gave us the candy."

"And we are going to take some stockings, and mittens, and picture books," Julia added.

"Flora and Julia and I bought the picture books with our own money," Molly went on; "and you can come with us, Priscilla, and carry one of the dolls. Aunt Mary and Ruth have to stay at home to get our Christmas tree ready. I must show you the dolls," and she opened the closet door with pride. "We haven't done them up yet. Here they are, all in a row. Aren't they sweet?"

The three dolls, like the Riley children, were of different sizes, making one think of a flight of steps. There was a strong family resemblance between them, for they all had flaxen hair and blue eyes. The oldest was dressed in red, and wore a red hood, which Molly's mamma had crocheted; the middle one was in blue, and had on a blue crocheted hood; and the youngest was in pink, and wore a pink hood.

"I wish they were all three mine," Priscilla said enviously.

"We have an engine and some cars for the little boy," said Molly, "and Miss Sylvia is going to give the big boys some jackknives. Here she comes now."

"So this is Priscilla," Miss Sylvia said cordially. "I feel as if we ought to be old friends, because I have heard so much about you from Molly."

continued

Priscilla looked hard at Miss Sylvia, and she did not wonder that Molly thought her like a fairy princess.

"We will do the dolls up in tissue paper," said Miss Sylvia. "Can't you find some, Molly, without troubling your aunt Mary? The other things are all ready, I see."

After the dolls were equipped for their journey, Miss Sylvia said:—

"You can carry the largest doll, Julia, because you are the oldest; and Priscilla can carry the middle-sized doll, and Molly can take the smallest."

Miss Sylvia carried the other presents in a basket, and Flora took some oranges and the bags of candy in another basket.

When they reached the Rileys' house, Miss Sylvia knocked on the door, and Mrs. Riley opened it.

"Oh, and is it you, Miss Sylvia?" she exclaimed. "Sure and you look like the blessed Saint Elizabeth."

"We have come to see the children," Miss Sylvia explained.

"They are all out in the field making believe they have a Christmas tree. I told them it was foolishness, for they haven't nothing to speak of to put on it."

Molly's eyes shone, and she ran off very fast in the direction of the field. How charming it would be to put real presents on a make-believe Christmas tree! For if it is always pleasant to "pretend," there is a certain satisfaction that comes from real things.

At first Molly could not see the Rileys, but at last she discovered them in the farther corner of the vacant lot, behind some hemlock-trees.

The snow had come early that year, and the sleet had fallen afterwards. There was a hard crust everywhere in the meadow, so that little people and big people too could walk on it as if it were ice.

When Molly and her friends reached the spot where the Rileys were playing, they became speechless with admiration, for before their astonished eyes was a whole miniature village. The buildings were all white, but so they often are in New England villages. Each house was made of blocks quarried out of the snow. There were open spaces for the doors and windows, as there are in blockhouses, and the children had put branches of hemlock inside, to look like green blinds and green doors. The roofs were all flat; they were made of pieces of wood about as large as the cover of a starch-box, put across the tops of the houses, and then covered with a thin layer of crust. Some diminutive snow chimneys crowned these structures. As for the church, it was very imposing, for it had a high tower and two wide doors. It stood near the common, a charming little round inclosure, fenced in by a hedge of tiny hemlock branches. The schoolhouse stood on one side of it and the village store on the other.

"I have never seen anything so beautiful," said Molly. "Did you make it yourselves?"

"Tom and Pat helped us."

"They were your architects, I suppose," said Miss Sylvia.

Tom and Pat, meanwhile, had retreated to the other end of the field.

The children were so entranced by the snow village that at first they did not notice the Christmas tree, but at length Priscilla pointed it out.

"Isn't it beautiful?" she asked.

"A real, live, out-of-doors Christmas tree growing in the fields. How perfectly lovely!" cried Molly.

"It isn't half so pretty as the house ones," cried Annie. "We didn't have any of them glistening balls, and we had to put on real snow instead of the make-believe kind."

"I think real snow is a great deal prettier," said Miss Sylvia.

It was a touching little Christmas tree, for it had tried so hard to copy its drawing-room sisters. The Rileys did not realize how pretty it looked out-of-doors, under the blue sky, with the real snow on its branches. There wasn't much else on them, to be sure, but there was a little of the crinkly barley candy that comes at Christmas time, tied on with some bits of bright ribbon; and there was a toy watch for the little boy; while some kindergarten mats that Katie had made at school, and some Christmas cards that had been given to the children the year before, helped to brighten up the sombre green branches. To add to the gayety of the scene, Priscilla the Second was frisking about, looking as white as the snow, and wearing a pretty blue ribbon around her neck.

"Suppose you children run off to the other end of the field for a few minutes," said Miss Sylvia to the little Rileys, "and we will call you when we want you."

After they had gone, Miss Sylvia and the children decorated the Christmas tree.

"I wish we had known that they were going to have a Christmas tree, and we would have brought some glistening balls," said Miss Sylvia.

"The candy bags and the other things will make it look very pretty," said Flora.

They tied the bags of candy to the branches of the tree.

"What shall we do with the oranges?" asked Molly.

"We'll put them in a ring around the bottom of the trunk of the tree," Julia decided.

So they arranged them in what Miss Sylvia called a fairy ring around the trunk, and then they hung the picture books over the branches.

"What shall we do with the mittens and stockings?" Flora asked in despair.

"We'll put them on the ends of the branches as if they were hands and feet," Miss Sylvia replied.

They left the train of cars just outside the village, and they seated the three dolls in front of three houses in the village.

"What can we do with the jackknives?" Molly inquired.

"We will put one jackknife in the lap of the doll in red, and the other in the lap of the doll in blue," said Julia.

When everything was ready, Julia and Molly ran to call the children.

"Ask the boys to come too," said Miss Sylvia.

Tom and Pat, however, had disappeared.

The little girls and the small Harry were very glad to follow Julia and Molly. When they saw the Christmas tree, they were as much overwhelmed with admiration as Molly had been when she saw the snow village. They did not say anything at first, but their eyes danced. At last Katie discovered the dolls. She gave a little cry of delight. "There are three of them."

"Yes," said Molly. "A big one, and a middle-sized one, and a little one. The youngest is for you."

"We made some of the clothes ourselves," Julia added proudly.

"The jackknives are for Tom and Pat," said Flora.

Katie, meanwhile, had seized the doll in pink, and clasped her in her arms as tenderly as if she had been alive. "What pretty hair she has," she said, "and such blue eyes. Sure and they shut up! Look, Annie, when you hold her this way they shut up."

"She's asleep," said Molly.

Annie was rapturously examining the doll in red, and Lizzie had taken blissful possession of the one in blue. The little boy had discovered the train of cars, and was already beginning to play with them.

"It will soon be dark," said Miss Sylvia, "and we must be going home, for we have a long walk."

Molly looked wistfully behind her. "I never saw anything so beautiful as this snow village," she said.

"Oh, that is nothing," Annie replied. "Any one can have a snow village. Snow is plenty."

Molly meant to try to make one in the garden at home, but she was sure that it would not be so beautiful.

"We thank you very much for all the things," said Annie shyly.

"We must really go now, Molly," Miss Sylvia insisted.

"Yes," added Flora, "we must get home in time for our own Christmas tree."

"It won't be like this one," said Molly regretfully.

"Nothing can be as beautiful as this." She wished that their Christmas tree was to be out-of-doors under the blue sky, with real snow on the branches, and that they could arrange it themselves, while Annie wished that she could have a Christmas tree in the house like Molly.

"We've had a lovely time," said Molly. "I never had such a lovely time before."

"Neither did we," Annie returned. "Good-by, and I wish you all a Merry Christmas." ♣

Spreading Holiday Cheer and Goodwill

Scores of angels broadcast it to the world on the night Christ was born. We sing about it in Christmas carols year after year. Every time you act on a kind feeling or express concern for someone, you are exercising it. Goodwill means reaching out to others and giving them a lift. It means sharing what you have with those who have not, whether it's a warm home, a loving family, planned festivities, or genuine friendship. And more often than not, the giver of the goodwill benefits as much, if not more, than the receiver.

Although most people typically direct their benevolent deeds at Christmas to family and close friends, just beyond those close-knit circles are many who long to share in the overflow of holiday goodwill. Far-from-home college students, singles of all ages, and elderly folks are grateful to be considered part of a family for a day or an evening. Others who would appreciate an outstretched hand are the needy; those in hospitals, nursing homes, or prisons; and anyone confined to a wheelchair or sickbed. If you're unsure whether someone would appreciate a kind gesture, go ahead and ask the person.

Entertain a group

Round up some amateur singers or actors and plan a visit to a hospital ward or nursing home to carol or put on a play. Before you go, call to make proper arrangements. Have copies of sheet music, lyrics, or scripts for the entertainers to refer to. Take along extra copies for the listeners. Arrive a few minutes early and don't stay too long. It's always nice to leave a little remembrance of your visit, too, such as cards, baked goods, or photos of your visit for the bulletin board.

Make a giant card

Another simple gesture that lifts spirits is delivering a giant homemade Christmas card. Use construction paper or, for a bigger card yet, two sides of a large cardboard box. Write a message and add decorations such as cutouts from previous years' Christmas cards. Get the whole family involved, and be sure to have everyone sign the card.

Cater to the worker

Here's an idea for cheering up anyone you know who has to work on Christmas Day. Pack a basketful of goodies or even an entire Christmas meal and take it to the jobsite to surprise the hard worker. Line the basket with a holiday tablecloth or napkins. Wrap breads or cakes in serving sizes to avoid the need to slice or cut them at work. Tuck in cheery notes and moist towelettes.

Feeding the Birds

Charity starts in a nest,
the human breast;
like birds
it needs no words
but sings
when it is given;
has wings
to lift
the spirit up,
by gift
of this small water cup,
to heaven;
and warm and light as feathers
    the bread spared
    to see creation fed.

Love in a crumb is a mystery;
bread is the Body of charity;
little nerves of finch or tit
fly down to feast and quicken it;
robin, blackbird, sparrow, wren,
feasted, quicken it in men.

—*Rumer Godden*

Be an escort

Being confined because of a disability or a lack of transportation causes many people to miss out on the wonderful sights and sounds of Christmas. If you know someone in this predicament, offer to be his or her wheels. Drive downtown to see the street decorations and store windows. Visit a local attraction decorated for the holidays, such as a historic mansion. For a special treat, take a guest to a Christmas program sponsored by a civic group or church.

Share family activities

Invite someone you know to take part in your family's traditional activities. Trimming the tree or even cutting or shopping for just the right one can put a lonely person in the holiday spirit. Offer to take someone without transportation Christmas shopping. Ask an elderly woman for her expert help in baking Christmas cookies. Set an extra place at the Christmas dinner table for a single person who might otherwise be celebrating alone.

Doctor up old toys

Have your kids gather together some of their toys they would want to give to kids who are less fortunate. Make any necessary repairs to restore them as close to their original state as you can. Wrap them individually, label them as to the contents or the age and sex of an appropriate recipient, and take them to a facility that can use them. Such places include prisons, for distribution to prisoners' families; hospitals, for use by pediatric patients; and centers for handicapped children. Before delivering the gifts, call to find out the needs and the feasibility of personally delivering the toys to the children. Many times, because of regulations, it's not possible to have personal contact with individuals in need. In fact, you may find it best to work through a local church or other charitable organization that has ongoing contact with the facility. ♠

Brunch For A Bunch

With Christmas approaching, get a group of merrymakers together on a frosty morning, and serve a hearty holiday brunch. Fortify the crowd before an afternoon assault on department stores or ski slopes with this snow-stopping make-ahead breakfast/lunch combination.

From left are *Buttermilk Doughnuts, Brunch Enchiladas, Cinnamon-Twist Coffee Cake,* and *Fresh Fruit with Apple Slush.* Recipes are on pages 176 and 177.

Cinnamon Twist Coffee Cake

If you're planning to make these coffee cakes in advance, freeze the coffee cakes before you add the icing. Then, when you're ready, thaw the coffee cakes and drizzle icing on them.

    1 package active dry yeast
 3¼ to 3¾ cups all-purpose
        flour
  ¾ cup milk
  ¼ cup butter *or* margarine
    3 tablespoons sugar
    1 teaspoon salt
    2 eggs
    3 tablespoons butter *or*
        margarine, melted
  ½ cup sugar
  ½ cup chopped walnuts
    2 teaspoons ground
        cinnamon

In a small mixer bowl combine yeast and *1½ cups* of flour. Heat together milk, ¼ cup butter or margarine, 3 tablespoons sugar, and salt till warm (110° to 115°) and butter is nearly melted. Add to yeast mixture; add eggs. Beat with an electric mixer on low speed for 30 seconds, scraping bowl. Beat for 3 minutes on high speed. By hand, stir in as much remaining flour as you can mix in with a spoon. On a floured surface knead in enough of the remaining flour to make a moderately stiff dough (5 to 8 minutes). Cover; let rise in a warm place till double (about 1½ hours).

Punch down; divide in half. Cover; let rest for 10 minutes. On a floured surface roll one half into a 20x9-inch rectangle. Spread *half* of the melted butter over dough. Combine ½ cup sugar, nuts, and cinnamon; sprinkle half over dough. Roll up jelly-roll style, beginning with long side. Seal edge. With a sharp knife, cut roll in half *lengthwise*, making two 20-inch portions. Place side by side with cut sides up. Moisten and press 2 ends of dough together several times by lifting 1 portion of dough over other. Shape into a ring in a greased 8-inch-round baking pan. Moisten ends and press together to seal. Repeat with remaining dough and filling. Cover; let rise till nearly double (about 45 minutes). Bake in a 350° oven about 25 minutes or till done. Let stand for 3 minutes. Loosen edges and transfer to serving plate. Makes 2.

Powdered Sugar Icing: In a small bowl combine 1 cup sifted *powdered sugar,* ¼ teaspoon *vanilla,* and enough *milk* to make icing of drizzling consistency. Drizzle over coffee cakes.

Fresh Fruit With Apple Slush

    3 cups apple juice *or*
        apple cider
    1 6-ounce can apricot nectar
  ½ of a 6-ounce can (⅓ cup)
        frozen lemonade
        concentrate
    1 10-ounce bottle ginger ale
    3 oranges
    3 bananas, sliced
  ½ pineapple, peeled and cut
        into cubes
    2 cups strawberries *or* halved
        red grapes

Stir together apple juice or apple cider, apricot nectar, and lemonade concentrate; stir till concentrate dissolves. Stir in ginger ale. Pour mixture into freezer container. Seal, label, and freeze.

Peel and section 2 oranges. Squeeze juice from other orange; reserve juice. Place oranges, bananas, pineapple, and strawberries in a serving bowl. Sprinkle with *sugar;* pour reserved orange juice over all. Chill for at least 2 hours.

Before serving, let frozen mixture stand at room temperature about 30 minutes or till partially thawed. Spoon fruit mixture into serving dishes; top with about ¼ cup frozen mixture. Reserve remaining frozen mixture for another use. Makes 10 servings.

Buttermilk Doughnuts

Dutch settlers introduced these little fried cakes to American pioneers, but it's a sea captain who is credited for the hole in the middle. Whether you like doughnuts with or without the hole, they're a simple way to sweeten the Christmas season.

3¼ cups all-purpose
    flour
1 teaspoon baking soda
½ teaspoon baking powder
½ teaspoon ground nutmeg
2 slightly beaten eggs
½ cup sugar
2 tablespoons butter *or*
    margarine, melted
1 cup buttermilk
    Shortening *or* cooking oil
    for deep-fat frying

In a mixing bowl stir together flour, baking soda, baking powder, nutmeg, and ⅛ teaspoon *salt;* set aside. In a large mixer bowl beat eggs and sugar till thick and lemon colored. Stir in melted butter or margarine. Add flour mixture and buttermilk alternately to egg mixture; beat just till combined after each addition. Cover; chill about 2 hours.

Turn the dough out onto a lightly floured surface. Roll to ½-inch thickness; cut with 2½-inch doughnut cutter. Fry in deep, hot fat (375°) about 1 minute per side or till golden, turning once. Drain on paper towels. While warm, sprinkle with additional *sugar or powdered sugar,* if desired. Makes 18 doughnuts.

Cranberry Ripple Cake

Perfect for holiday happenings, this festive cake can be made in place of the Cinnamon-Twist Coffee Cake. Or, serve both at your brunch.

2 cups all-purpose flour
1 teaspoon baking powder
1 teaspoon baking soda
½ cup butter *or* margarine
1 cup sugar
½ teaspoon almond extract
2 eggs
1 8-ounce carton dairy sour
    cream
1 8-ounce can whole
    cranberry sauce
½ cup chopped pecans

In a mixing bowl stir together flour, baking powder, soda, and ¼ teaspoon *salt.* In a large mixer bowl beat butter or margarine for 30 seconds. Add sugar and extract; beat till fluffy. Add eggs; beat well. Add flour mixture and sour cream alternately to creamed mixture, beating after each addition till smooth.

Spread *half* of the batter in a greased and floured 10-inch tube pan. Spoon *½ cup* of cranberry sauce over batter. Spoon remaining batter over sauce, spreading as much as possible. Top with remaining cranberry sauce. Sprinkle pecans atop. Bake in a 350° oven for 40 to 50 minutes. Cool for 10 minutes. Remove from pan; cool on a wire rack. Makes 1.

Brunch Enchiladas

This cheesy make-ahead main dish is perfect for busy party planners.

    Cornmeal
12 ounces (2 cups) ground
    fully cooked ham
1½ cups shredded cheddar
    cheese (6 ounces)
½ cup sliced green onion
1 4-ounce can chopped chili
    peppers, drained
8 7-inch flour tortillas
4 beaten eggs
2 cups light cream
1 tablespoon all-purpose
    flour
¼ teaspoon garlic powder
    Few drops bottled hot
    pepper sauce
1 cup shredded cheddar
    cheese (4 ounces)

Grease a 12x7½x2-inch baking dish. Sprinkle with cornmeal; set aside. In a mixing bowl combine ground ham, 1½ cups cheese, onion, and chili peppers. Place ⅓ cup of the mixture at one end of each tortilla; roll up. Arrange tortillas, seam side down, in prepared dish.

In a mixing bowl stir together eggs, cream, flour, garlic powder, and hot pepper sauce; pour over tortillas. Cover and chill for 4 hours or overnight. Bake, covered, in a 350° oven for 55 to 60 minutes or till set. Sprinkle with 1 cup cheese; let stand for 10 minutes. Makes 8 servings.

Canapés For A Crowd

Spread Christmas cheer
this holiday season
by opening your home to
a convivial group of
friends and neighbors.
Invite chums to a festive
open house, and watch
Christmas spirits soar.
With this tempting array
of finger foods, your
yuletide guests can mingle
and nibble at the
same time.

Clockwise, from top left, are
*Appeteaser Pie, Beer-Cheese Pinecones,
Turkey Pâté, Salmon-Stuffed Pasta
Shells, International Sandwich Board,*
and *Cranberry-Cinnamon Punch.*
Recipes are on pages 180–182.

International Sandwich Board

12 ounces lean boneless pork
15 wonton skins, halved diagonally
    Finely shredded Chinese cabbage *or* green cabbage
    Crushed pineapple (juice pack), drained
    Bottled sweet and sour sauce
    Unpeeled apple slices
    Lemon juice
1 8-ounce package (36) crisp rye crackers
3 4-ounce containers whipped cream cheese
1 8-ounce jar pickled herring, drained
    Fresh dill (optional)
1 package pumpernickel party bread rounds
    Butter *or* margarine
1 16-ounce can mayonnaise-style potato salad, chilled
1 6-ounce can pickled sliced beets, well drained
    Sieved hard-cooked egg
    Caviar (optional)
½ cup chopped chutney
½ teaspoon curry powder
2 2½-ounce packages thinly sliced pressed chicken, snipped
    Water wafer crackers
    Raisins, chopped peanuts, *or* shredded coconut

Oriental Sandwiches: Partially freeze pork; slice thinly across the grain into bite-size strips. Stir-fry pork in a small amount of hot oil about 2 minutes or till no longer pink. Drain. In a large skillet heat oil for shallow-fat frying to 365°. Fry wonton skins, a few at a time, till golden. Drain well on paper towels. Top each with shredded cabbage, pineapple, pork, and sweet and sour sauce. Makes 30.

Scandinavian Sandwiches: Dip apple slices in a mixture of lemon juice and water. Spread rye crackers with cream cheese; top each cracker with some pickled herring and an apple slice. Garnish with fresh dill, if desired. Makes 36.

Russian Sandwiches: Spread pumpernickel bread rounds with butter; top with *1 tablespoon* potato salad. Place a slice of beet atop. Garnish with egg and caviar, if desired. Makes about 32.

Indian Sandwiches: Stir together chutney and curry; stir in chicken. Spoon the mixture onto crackers. Garnish with raisins, peanuts, or coconut. Makes about 32.

Salmon-Stuffed Pasta Shells

1 8-ounce package (25 to 30) conch-shaped pasta shells
2 beaten eggs
2 cups ricotta cheese
½ cup finely chopped green pepper
¼ cup finely chopped onion
¼ cup snipped parsley
¼ cup milk *or* light cream
½ teaspoon finely shredded lemon peel
½ teaspoon salt
¼ teaspoon ground mace
1 15½-ounce can salmon, drained, flaked, and skin and bones removed
⅓ cup fine dry bread crumbs
⅓ cup grated Parmesan cheese
2 tablespoons butter *or* margarine, melted

Cook pasta shells, uncovered, in a large amount of lightly salted boiling water about 20 minutes or just till tender; drain. Rinse with cold water; drain. Set aside.

In a bowl combine eggs, ricotta cheese, green pepper, onion, parsley, milk, lemon peel, salt, and mace. Stir in salmon. Spoon mixture into cooked shells. Place shells, filled side up, in a 13x9x2-inch baking dish; add 2 tablespoons *water*. Cover; bake in a 350° oven for 30 minutes. In a bowl combine bread crumbs, Parmesan cheese, and butter; sprinkle over shells. Bake, uncovered, for 5 minutes more. Serve hot. Makes 25 to 30.

Turkey Pâté

A perfect use for leftover turkey!

½ cup finely chopped carrot
½ cup finely chopped celery
⅓ cup finely chopped onion
2 tablespoons cooking oil
⅓ cup dry white wine
2 teaspoons dried dillweed
1 teaspoon drained capers, finely chopped
3 cups ground cooked turkey
½ cup finely chopped pine nuts *or* almonds
2 hard-cooked eggs, chopped
   Leaf lettuce
   Assorted crackers *or* party bread rounds

In a large saucepan cook carrot, celery, and onion in hot oil till tender but not brown. Remove from the heat. Stir in wine, 1 teaspoon *salt,* dillweed, capers, and ¼ teaspoon *pepper.* Add turkey, nuts, and hard-cooked eggs.

Transfer *one-fourth* of the mixture to a blender container or food processor bowl. Blend or process till smooth. Repeat with remaining mixture, one-fourth at a time. Turn mixture into an oiled 4-cup mold. Cover; chill in the refrigerator for several hours or overnight. Unmold pâté onto a lettuce-lined serving plate. If desired, garnish the plate with carrot flowers, carrot curls, and celery fans. Serve pâté with crackers or bread. Makes 3½ cups spread.

Beer-Cheese Pinecones

2 8-ounce packages cream cheese, softened
½ cup beer
2 tablespoons finely snipped parsley
1 teaspoon paprika
3 cups shredded smoked sharp cheddar cheese (12 ounces)
   Sliced almonds
   Pear slices (optional)
   Apple slices (optional)
   Assorted crackers (optional)

In a large bowl beat together cream cheese, beer, parsley, and paprika until well mixed. Stir in the cheddar cheese. Cover and chill mixture for 1 hour.

Divide mixture in half. Mold each half into a pinecone shape; place on a baking sheet. Insert sliced almonds in rows over cheese to resemble pinecones.

Cover and chill for several hours. To serve, transfer pinecones to a board or platter with a wide metal spatula. Serve spread with pear slices, apple slices, and assorted crackers, if desired. Makes about 4 cups spread.

Appeteaser Pie

A wedge of this hot, flaky appetizer pie will tease any appetite.

1 package (8) refrigerated crescent rolls
1 8-ounce carton dairy sour cream
1 3-ounce package cream cheese with chives, softened
1 tablespoon snipped parsley
1½ teaspoons fines herbes
   Assorted toppings: halved red *or* green pepper rings; halved sliced cucumber; sliced pitted ripe olive; sliced hard-cooked eggs; drained, canned shrimp

Unroll crescent roll dough; separate into triangles. On a 12-inch ungreased pizza pan, evenly space the triangles in a spoke fashion, with the points toward the center, to form a circle. Press to seal seams and cover bottom and sides of pan. Flute edge, if desired.

Bake in a 375° oven about 10 minutes or till light brown. In a small bowl stir sour cream into cream cheese till smooth. Stir in parsley and fines herbes. Spread over crust. Starting from the outside edge, arrange toppings in a circular design atop cream cheese layer. Bake for 7 to 8 minutes more or till heated through. Serve warm. Cut into wedges. Makes 12 appetizer servings.

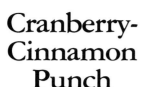

Cranberry-Cinnamon Punch

2 cups fresh cranberries
8 cups water
½ cup sugar
¼ cup red cinnamon candies
3 whole cloves
½ cup orange juice
2 tablespoons lemon juice
   Orange *or* lemon slices,
      quartered (optional)

Wash the cranberries. In a large saucepan stir together cranberries with *3 cups* of water. Bring mixture to boiling; reduce the heat. Simmer, uncovered, about 5 minutes or till cranberry skins pop. Remove from the heat; cool.

Press cranberries through a food mill or sieve. Strain cranberry juice through several layers of cheesecloth to remove the small seeds.

In a 4½-quart Dutch oven or kettle combine cranberry juice, remaining 5 cups water, sugar, cinnamon candies, and cloves. Bring to boiling; reduce the heat. Boil gently for 5 minutes, stirring to dissolve candies. Stir in orange juice and lemon juice. Serve hot or cold. Garnish each serving with orange or lemon slices, if desired. Makes 10 (6-ounce) servings.

Quick Champagne Punch

Chill the beverage ingredients ahead, then combine all the ingredients in the punch bowl just before guests arrive. For a dazzling presentation, trim the base of your punch bowl with a grapevine wreath and tiny lights or ornaments.

1 6-ounce can frozen
   lemonade concentrate
1 750-ml bottle champagne
2¾ cups unsweetened
   pineapple juice
2 cups club soda
1½ cups dry white wine
2 cups vanilla ice cream

In a large bowl prepare lemonade according to can directions. Add champagne, pineapple juice, club soda, and wine. Top with scoops of vanilla ice cream. Stir gently before serving. Makes about 32 (4-ounce) servings.

Eggnog

For eggnog without the spirits, prepare Eggnog as directed, except omit the bourbon and rum and increase the milk to 2 cups.

3 egg whites
½ cup sugar
3 egg yolks
1 cup whipping cream
1 cup milk
1 cup bourbon
1 tablespoon dark rum
   Freshly grated nutmeg *or*
      ground nutmeg

In a large mixer bowl beat egg whites till soft peaks form (tips curl). Gradually add ¼ cup sugar, beating till stiff peaks form (tips stand straight). Set aside.

In a small mixer bowl beat egg yolks till thick and lemon colored. Gradually beat in the remaining sugar. Fold egg yolk mixture into beaten egg whites. Stir in whipping cream, milk, bourbon, and rum. Cover and chill.

Before serving, sprinkle with nutmeg. Makes about 12 servings.

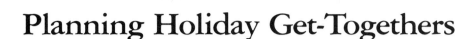

Planning Holiday Get-Togethers

Christmastime is party time. Celebrate the holiday season this year with a gala gathering for friends, neighbors, or the gang at work. Here are some tips to help assure that all of your yuletide entertaining comes off without a hitch.

Social setting
Begin with the guest list. Share the spirit of the season with a congenial group of chums—whether it's five or 50. Then, simply tailor your plans to fit the number of guests. If the list is long, consider a glittery open house (see the party recipes on pages 180–182) or an old-fashioned potluck. For a smaller group, you might want to plan an elaborate sit-down dinner or a festive brunch (see the brunch recipes on pages 178 and 179).

Inviting invitations
During the Christmas season, people are busy shopping, baking, and visiting friends, so telephone or mail your invitations early. Make sure you provide all of the necessary information: date, time, place, type of party, attire (if special), address, phone number, and an RSVP request so you'll know how many people to expect. If you mail invitations, choose ones that reflect the style of your party and the time of the year. Include a map for those who need one. If you phone, call everyone on the same day so none of your guests will feel they're an afterthought.

Menu magic
Making sure everything goes smoothly doesn't have to mean long hours in the kitchen.
- Plan menus that blend foods you're comfortable with and one or two new dishes you think guests will like.
- Avoid foods that are the same color. Serve dishes that have different textures and tastes, too. Try combining sweet foods and salty ones, bland dishes and spicy ones.
- Work as many make-ahead foods as you can into your menu. That way, you'll have more time for decking the halls, hanging mistletoe, and stuffing stockings before guests arrive.

Greeting guests
A cheerful welcome at the door is sure to put guests in the Christmas spirit and let them know how much you value their coming. Introductions, when necessary, make guests feel more at ease. Have refreshments on tables that are easy to get to. If you allow smoking in your house, provide plenty of ashtrays. Light a few candles to clear the air for nonsmokers and perhaps crack a window to allow fresh air to circulate. Add a few festive touches to the guest bathroom, too—a small evergreen wreath, scented soaps, and bright guest towels, for example.

Seasonal settings
Let your style and the occasion create the table setting for your celebration. If you prefer the natural look, collect evergreen branches, pinecones, and holly for a centerpiece. If you like nostalgia, visit antique shops and come away with Christmas knickknacks from days gone by. For a simple setting, you can use a poinsettia and some ornaments. Anything goes. For serving pieces and place settings, use holiday paper plates and napkins or your finest china, depending on the type of party and the number of guests.

Enjoying yourself
Now, with all your party planning done, you're set to join in all the holiday fun. Relax, mingle with your guests, and enjoy! ♣

Welcome Here!

I've got a pie all baked complete,
Pudding too, that's very sweet.
Chestnuts are roasting, join us here
While we dance and make good cheer.

I've got a log that's burning hot,
Toddy's bubbling in the pot.
Come in, ye people, where it's warm,
The wind blows sharp and it may storm.

I made a loaf that's cooling there,
With my neighbors, I will share.
Come, all ye people, hear me sing
A song of friendly welcoming.

Welcome here, welcome here,
all be alive and be of good cheer.
Welcome here, welcome here,
all be alive and be of good cheer.

HOLIDAY DATEBOOK

1987
NOVEMBER

Thursday 26 ■ **Thanksgiving Day** (United States)

Friday 27

Saturday 28

Sunday 29

Monday 30

DECEMBER

Tuesday 1

Wednesday 2

Thursday 3

Friday 4

Saturday 5

DECEMBER

Sunday 6	
Monday 7	
Tuesday 8	
Wednesday 9	
Thursday 10	
Friday 11	
Saturday 12	
Sunday 13	
Monday 14	
Tuesday 15	
Wednesday 16	
Thursday 17	
Friday 18	
Saturday 19	

Sunday **20**	
Monday **21**	
Tuesday **22**	
Wednesday **23**	
Thursday **24**	■ **Christmas Eve**
Friday **25**	■ **Christmas Day**
Saturday **26**	
Sunday **27**	
Monday **28**	■ **Boxing Day (Canada)**
Tuesday **29**	
Wednesday **30**	
Thursday **31**	
	JANUARY
Friday **1**	■ **New Year's Day**
Saturday **2**	

ACKNOWLEDGMENTS

Editor: Marsha Jahns
Designers: Randall A. Yontz, Mike Burns
Contributing Writers: Debra Felton,
Jill Johnson, Maureen Powers, Martha Schiel

We extend our thanks and appreciation to the many people who granted us permission to use their stories, poems, songs, and illustrations in this book.

Pages 10–13: "The Peterkins' Christmas-Tree" by Lucretia P. Hale reprinted from THE PETERKIN PAPERS by Lucretia P. Hale, published by Houghton-Mifflin, 1886.

Pages 26–31: "December" by Elizabeth Coatsworth reprinted with permission of Macmillan Publishing Company from TWELVE MONTHS MAKE A YEAR by Elizabeth Coatsworth. Copyright © 1943 by Macmillan Publishing Company, renewed 1971 by Elizabeth Coatsworth Beston.

Page 45: "Winter Sports" from THE GIANT CHRISTMAS BOOK by Lenore Hetrick. Copyright © 1934 by Lurten M. Paine, Paine Publishing Company, Dayton, Ohio.

Page 46–47: The illustration "Deadman's Hill" by Norman Rockwell. Copyright © Brown & Bigelow USA 1957. All rights reserved.

Page 47: "Look at the Snow" by Mary Carolyn Davies from Child Life Magazine, Copyright © 1937, 1965 by Rand McNally & Company.

Page 60–63: "Once on Christmas" by Dorothy Thompson. Copyright © 1938 by Dorothy Thompson. Used by permission of The Estate of Michael Lewis.

Page 74–77: "The Gift of the Magi" by O. Henry. Copyright © 1905 by The World from THE COMPLETE WORKS OF O. HENRY. Reprinted by permission of Doubleday & Company, Inc.

Pages 78–79: The illustration "American Winter Scenes. Morning" by Currier and Ives courtesy of The Harry T. Peters Collection, Museum of the City of New York.

Pages 80–81: The illustration "Early Winter" by Currier and Ives courtesy of The Harry T. Peters Collection, Museum of the City of New York.

Page: 81: "Christmas Wish" by Elizabeth Searle Lamb, by permission of the author.

Pages 82–83: The illustration "American Winter Scenes. Morning" by Currier and Ives courtesy of The Harry T. Peters Collection, Museum of the City of New York.

Page 83: "Mistletoe Sprites" by Solveig Paulson Russell. Reprinted by permission of the author's daughter, Brenda Russell.

Pages 84–85: The illustration "Winter in the Country. A Cold Morning" by Currier and Ives courtesy of The Harry T. Peters Collection, Museum of the City of New York.

Page 91: "Tiny Tim" by Norman Rockwell reprinted by permission of Thomas Rockwell.

Page 96–99: "Suzanne's Own Night" by Bess Streeter Aldrich from JOURNEY INTO CHRISTMAS AND OTHER STORIES by Bess Streeter Aldrich. Copyright 1949 by Appleton-Century-Crofts, Inc., renewed 1977 by Mary Aldrich Beechner, Robert Streeter Aldrich, Charles S. Aldrich, and James Whitson Aldrich. A Hawthorn book. Reprinted by permission of E.P. Dutton, a division of New American Library.

Page 102: excerpt from THE LITTLE PRINCE by Antoine de Saint Exupéry reprinted by permission of the publisher, Harcourt Brace Jovanovich, Inc.

Page 115: "To Louis at Christmas" by Ilien Coffey is reprinted by permission from CHRISTMAS, An American Annual of Christmas Literature and Art, Vol. 52, copyright © 1982 Augsburg Publishing House.

Pages 116–119: "White Christmas" by Alice Dalgliesh reprinted with permission of Macmillan Publishing Company from THE BLUE TEAPOT by Alice Dalgliesh. Copyright © 1931 by Macmillan Publishing Company, renewed 1959 by Alice Dalgliesh.

Pages 126–127: "The Christmas Tree Lamb" by
Kathryn Jackson from THE ANIMALS' MERRY
CHRISTMAS copyright © 1950 Western Publishing
Company, Inc. Used by permission.

Page 129: "Merry Christmas" from CHRISTMAS,
edited by Robert Haven Schauffler.

Pages 142–144: "The Year We Had a Sensible
Christmas" by Henry Appers reprinted with permission
from Guideposts magazine. Copyright © 1964 by
Guideposts Associates, Inc., Carmel, New York 10512.

Pages 156–159: "Tilly's Christmas" by Louisa M.
Alcott from A BOOK OF CHRISTMAS STORIES
FOR CHILDREN by Maude Owens Walters, published
by Dodd, Mead & Company, Inc.

Pages 168–171: "The Rileys' Christmas Tree" by Eliza
Orne White reprinted from WHEN MOLLY WAS SIX
by Eliza Orne White, published by Houghton-Mifflin,
1894.

Page 173: "Feeding the Birds" by Rumer Godden
reprinted by permission of Rumer Godden from THE
DOLL'S BOUQUET, a magazine for dolls by Tasha
Tudor.

Page 184: " Welcome Here!" from THE SEASON
FOR SINGING by John Langstaff. Copyright © 1974
by John M. Langstaff. Reprinted by permission of
Doubleday & Company, Inc.

*Our special thanks to the following photographers and
illustrators, who generously contributed their creative talents
and expertise to this book.*

Pages 2–3: Robert Cushman Hayes

Pages 8–9: Robert Cushman Hayes

Page 11: Helen K. Kunze

Page 13: Helen K. Kunze

Page 22: Perry Struse

Page 25: Perry Struse

Page 27: Robert Cushman Hayes

Page 40: John Kelly

Pages 58–59: Vaughn Winchell

Page 61: Robert Cushman Hayes

Page 75: Helen K. Kunze

Page 77: Helen K. Kunze

Pages 86–87: William Hopkins

Page 95: William Hopkins

Pages 100–101: Robert Cushman Hayes

Pages 102–103: Helen K. Kunze

Page 104: Bob Taylor

Page 117: Robert Cushman Hayes

Page 126: William Hopkins

Pages 128–129: Perry Struse

Page 131: Perry Struse

Page 133: Helen K. Kunze

Page 142: Helen K. Kunze

Page 157: Helen K. Kunze

Page 159: Helen K. Kunze

INDEX

HOLIDAY GET-TOGETHER RECIPES

Family, friends, delicious food, and warm hospitality. These are the ingredients for memorable holiday get-togethers. On the pages that follow, you'll find four festive party ideas: a tree-trimming party, Christmas Eve buffet, skating party, and cookie exchange. We know these recipes, celebration hints, and inspiring photographs will give you many ideas for planning great food and great times during the holidays. Just add family and friends, then enjoy!

Tree-Trimming Party

Share the joy and fun of trimming your tree with your family, friends, and neighbors. Ask the kids to do something special by making a cookie ornament to add to the tree or take home for their own tree (see recipe, page 203).

Swedish Meatballs

1 beaten egg
⅓ cup light cream
1 cup soft bread crumbs
⅓ cup finely chopped onion
2 tablespoons snipped
   parsley
¾ teaspoon salt
⅛ teaspoon ground nutmeg
½ pound ground veal
½ pound lean ground pork
1 tablespoon butter *or*
   margarine
1 tablespoon all-purpose
   flour
1 teaspoon instant chicken
   bouillon granules
⅛ teaspoon ground nutmeg
1¾ cups light cream

In a mixing bowl combine the egg and the ⅓ cup cream. Stir in the bread crumbs, onion, parsley, salt, and ⅛ teaspoon nutmeg. Add the ground veal and pork; mix well. Shape the meat mixture into 48 meatballs. Place the meatballs in a 15x10x1-inch baking pan. Bake in a 350° oven about 20 minutes or till the meatballs are no longer pink in the center.

Meanwhile, for sauce, in a saucepan melt the butter or margarine. Stir in the flour, bouillon granules, and ⅛ teaspoon nutmeg. Stir in the 1¾ cups light cream. Cook and stir till the sauce is thickened and bubbly. Cook and stir for 2 minutes more. Drain the meatballs; combine with the sauce and transfer to a serving bowl. Makes 48 meatballs.

Scandinavian Appetizer Tray

Swedish Meatballs (see
   recipe at left)
½ pound potato sausage *or*
   Polish sausage
¼ cup water
1 tablespoon cooking oil
1 pint pickled herring,
   chilled
1 medium cucumber, sliced
   Dill pickle slices
   Leaf lettuce

Prepare the Swedish Meatballs; keep warm. Pierce the sausage with a fork in several places. Place the sausage links in a skillet; add the water. Bring to boiling. Cover and simmer for 5 minutes; drain well. Add the oil to the skillet. Cook slowly, uncovered, for 12 to 14 minutes more or till the liquid from the sausage has evaporated and sausage is thoroughly cooked.

Slice the sausage into ½-inch-thick slices. Then, arrange the sausage, herring, cucumber slices, and pickle slices on a serving tray lined with leaf lettuce. Spoon the meatballs into a heat-proof bowl and place in the center of the tray. Garnish the appetizer tray with fresh dill, if desired. Makes 8 to 10 appetizer servings.

Sherry-Cheese Log

1 8-ounce package
   Neufchâtel cheese
1½ cups shredded Swiss cheese
   (6 ounces)
1 tablespoon snipped parsley
2 tablespoons cream sherry
⅓ cup chopped almonds,
   toasted (optional)
   Snipped parsley
   Sesame seed, toasted
   Assorted crackers

Let the Neufchâtel and Swiss cheeses stand at room temperature for 1 hour. In a small mixer bowl beat the cheeses and the 1 tablespoon parsley till combined. Gradually add the cream sherry, beating till nearly smooth. Stir in the almonds, if desired. Cover and chill for 1 hour.

With your hands, mold the mixture into a 10-inch-long log shape. Press additional snipped parsley and sesame seed onto the cheese log, forming decorative rows of each.

Wrap the log in moisture-vaporproof wrap. Chill. Or, seal, label, and freeze, if desired. If the cheese log is frozen, let it thaw for 1½ to 2 hours at room temperature. Unwrap. Serve the cheese log on a platter with assorted crackers; garnish with red grapes, if desired. Makes 10 servings.

Chicken-Stuffed Cream Puffs

½ cup water
¼ cup butter *or* margarine
½ cup all-purpose flour
2 eggs
½ cup shredded Muenster *or* Swiss cheese (2 ounces)
1 5-ounce can boned white chicken, drained and flaked
½ cup finely chopped water chestnuts
¼ cup buttermilk salad dressing with chives *or* mayonnaise *or* salad dressing
1 2-ounce can mushroom stems and pieces, drained and chopped
1 tablespoon chopped pimiento
¼ teaspoon dry mustard

In a 2-quart saucepan bring the ½ cup water and the butter or margarine to boiling. Add the flour; stir vigorously. Cook and stir till the mixture forms a ball that doesn't separate. Remove from the heat; cool for 10 minutes. Add the eggs, one at a time, beating for 1 minute after each addition or till smooth. Stir in cheese. Spoon mixture into a pastry bag fitted with a decorative tip. Pipe batter into spirals, 1 inch in diameter, onto a greased baking sheet. Or, using 1 rounded teaspoon dough for each puff, drop dough onto a greased baking sheet. Bake in a 400° oven about 20 minutes or till puffed. Remove from the oven; cut off tops. Remove any soft dough. Cool puffs on a wire rack. If de-sired, store puffs, tightly covered, up to 1 day at room temperature. Or, cover tightly with moisture-vaporproof wrap; freeze. Let thaw for 1 hour at room temperature.

For filling, combine chicken, water chestnuts, salad dressing, mushrooms, pimiento, and mustard. Cover; chill. Spoon the chicken filling into the puff bottoms; replace tops. To serve, garnish with parsley sprigs, if desired. Makes 28 puffs.

Swiss Cheese Bites

3 cups shredded process Swiss cheese (12 ounces)
⅔ cup shortening
1½ cups all-purpose flour
3 tablespoons cold water

Bring the cheese to room temperature. In a mixer bowl combine the cheese and shortening; beat with an electric mixer on medium speed till nearly smooth. Stir in the flour. Sprinkle *1 tablespoon* of the water over part of the mixture; toss with a fork. Push to the side of the bowl. Repeat till all is moistened. Shape into 1-inch balls or 1½x½-inch sticks. Place on a lightly greased baking sheet. Bake in a 375° oven for 20 to 25 minutes or till light brown. Cool on wire racks. Makes about 60.

Toasted Ravioli With Red Sauce

1 large bag (26½ ounces) frozen meat *or* cheese ravioli without sauce
¾ cup fine dry bread crumbs
1 tablespoon snipped parsley
½ teaspoon garlic powder
¼ cup milk
Cooking oil for deep-fat frying
½ cup grated Parmesan cheese
Red Sauce

Cook ravioli according to package directions. Combine crumbs, parsley, garlic powder, and ½ teaspoon *salt*. Drain ravioli; pat dry. Cool. Dip ravioli, a few at a time, in milk. Toss with crumb mixture. Fry, a few at a time, in hot oil (365°) for 30 seconds; drain on paper towels. Chill. Arrange on a baking sheet in a single layer. Sprinkle cheese atop. Bake in a 350° oven about 15 minutes or till heated through. Serve with Red Sauce. Makes about 50.

RED SAUCE: Drain one 14½-ounce can *Italian-style tomatoes*, reserving the tomato juice. Seed and coarsely chop the tomatoes. Set aside. Cook 1 medium *onion*, chopped, and 1 clove *garlic*, minced, in 2 tablespoons *olive oil* till tender but not brown. Stir in tomatoes; reserved tomato juice; ⅓ cup *tomato paste*; ½ teaspoon *salt*; ½ teaspoon dried *basil*, crushed; and ¼ teaspoon *sugar*. Bring to boiling. Reduce the heat and simmer, uncovered, about 30 minutes or till desired consistency, stirring occasionally.

Shrimp and Havarti Pastries

1 package piecrust mix for
   2-crust pie
½ cup dairy sour cream
½ cup finely chopped onion
1 clove garlic
1 tablespoon cooking oil
2 teaspoons all-purpose flour
⅓ cup milk
¾ cup shredded havarti
   cheese (3 ounces)
8 ounces frozen peeled and
   deveined shrimp, cooked
   and finely chopped
   Milk

Stir together piecrust mix and sour cream with a fork till blended. If the dough is dry, add 1 tablespoon *milk.* Form into a ball. Cover and chill. Cook onion and garlic in oil till tender but not brown. Stir in flour. Add milk all at once. Cook and stir till thickened and bubbly. Cook and stir for 1 minute more. Add cheese; stir till melted. Remove from the heat. Stir in chopped shrimp.

   Divide dough into quarters. On a floured surface roll each quarter to about 1/16-inch thickness. With a floured cutter, cut into 3-inch circles. Spoon about 1 teaspoon shrimp mixture onto half of each circle. Fold in half; seal edge with the tines of a fork. Repeat with the remaining dough and filling. Prick tops. Brush with milk. Bake on an ungreased baking sheet in a 400° oven for 15 minutes. Makes about 42.

Christmas Cheer Recipe

Take a bushel of tinsel, sprinkle well throughout the house. Add two dozen stars and one graceful Christmas tree. Take a generous spray of mistletoe, an armload of holly and a full measure of snow laid in curved hills along the window sills. Toss in a Christmas carol, and season well with good will and friendly laughter. Light the candles, "one for adoration, two for celebration." Let the first burn brightly, and may those you love be near.
The yield: One Happy Christmas
—*Clementine Paddleford*

Antipasto Pizza

1 4-ounce package thinly
   sliced salami
2½ to 3 cups all-purpose flour
1 package active dry yeast
1 cup warm water (115° to
   120°)
2 tablespoons cooking oil
2 cups shredded mozzarella
   cheese (8 ounces)
4 medium tomatoes, sliced
1 green pepper, sliced
1 8-ounce jar pickled
   mushrooms, drained and
   halved
¼ teaspoon dried basil,
   crushed
¼ cup grated Parmesan
   cheese
10 pitted large ripe olives

Remove 10 slices of salami from
the package; set aside. Finely chop
remaining salami to make about ½
cup. In a large mixer bowl combine *1¼ cups* of the flour, the
yeast, and chopped salami. Add
warm water and oil. Beat with an
electric mixer on low speed for ½
minute, scraping sides of the bowl
constantly. Beat 3 minutes on high
speed. Stir in as much of the remaining flour as you can mix in
with a spoon. Turn the dough out
onto a lightly floured surface.
Knead in enough of the remaining flour to make a moderately
stiff dough that is smooth and elastic (6 to 8 minutes). Cover; let rest
for 10 minutes.

Divide the dough in half. On a
lightly floured surface roll each
half into a 13-inch circle. Transfer
circles to greased 12-inch pizza
pans or baking sheets. Build up
edges slightly. Bake in a 425°
oven for 15 to 20 minutes or till
lightly browned. Sprinkle crusts
with shredded cheese. Arrange tomato, green pepper, and mushrooms on crusts. Sprinkle basil
over tomatoes. Sprinkle all with
Parmesan cheese.

Return to the 425° oven; bake
about 10 minutes longer or till
hot. Form reserved salami slices
into cones; fold tips under. Place
an olive in each. Arrange, spoke
fashion, in the center of the pizzas,
points toward the center. Makes
24 appetizer servings.

Artichoke-Chili Dip

1 14-ounce can artichoke
   hearts, drained
   and chopped
1 cup grated Parmesan
   cheese
1 cup mayonnaise *or* salad
   dressing
1 4-ounce can green chili
   peppers, rinsed, seeded,
   and chopped
   Tortilla chips

In a mixing bowl combine the artichoke hearts, Parmesan cheese,
mayonnaise or salad dressing, and
chili peppers. Spoon the mixture
into an 8x1½-inch round baking
dish. Bake in a 350° oven about
20 minutes or till heated through.
Serve warm with tortilla chips.
Makes about 2⅔ cups.

Romano-and-Shrimp-Stuffed Mushrooms

20 large fresh mushrooms
   (2 to 2½ inches in
   diameter)
1 4½-ounce can shrimp,
   drained, rinsed, and
   chopped
1 4-ounce container whipped
   cream cheese with chives
½ teaspoon Worcestershire
   sauce
   Dash garlic powder
   Dash bottled hot pepper
   sauce
   Grated Romano cheese

Remove the stems from the mushrooms; save for another use. Simmer the mushroom caps in boiling
water for 2 minutes. Drain; invert
caps on paper towels. Cool. Meanwhile, combine the shrimp, cream
cheese, Worcestershire sauce, garlic powder, and hot pepper sauce.
Spoon the shrimp mixture into the
mushroom caps; place in a shallow
baking pan or dish. Sprinkle with
the Romano cheese. Cover; chill
for 3 to 24 hours. Before serving,
uncover; bake in a 400° oven
about 15 minutes or till heated
through. Makes 20.

Ham-Pineapple Nibbles

These easy-to-make pastries start with crescent rolls and ground ham.

- 2 packages (8 rolls each) refrigerated crescent rolls
- 1 slightly beaten egg
- 1 8¼-ounce can crushed pineapple, drained
- ¼ cup soft bread crumbs
- 2 tablespoons sliced green onion
- ¼ teaspoon ground sage
- 1½ cups ground fully cooked ham
- ½ cup shredded mozzarella cheese *or* shredded cheddar cheese (2 ounces)

Separate crescent rolls into 8 rectangles. Pinch diagonal seams together. Pat or roll each rectangle to about 8x4 inches. Cut each rectangle crosswise into thirds.

In a mixing bowl stir together the egg, drained pineapple, bread crumbs, green onion, and sage. Stir in the ground ham and shredded cheese. Place *one rounded tablespoon* of the ham mixture on one end of *each* dough rectangle.

Fold other end of dough over filling. Seal with the tines of a fork. Place on an ungreased baking sheet and bake in a 375° oven for 10 to 13 minutes or till golden brown. Makes 24.

Curried Nuts

- 3 tablespoons butter *or* margarine
- 1½ teaspoons Worcestershire sauce
- 1 teaspoon curry powder
- 1½ cups pecan halves
- 1½ cups raw peanuts

In a large saucepan melt the butter or margarine. Stir in the Worcestershire sauce and curry powder. Add the pecan halves and peanuts; stir well to evenly coat the nuts.

Spread the mixture evenly in a shallow baking pan. Bake in a 300° oven for 15 to 20 minutes or till lightly toasted, stirring once. Remove from the oven. Cool. Makes 3 cups.

Cheese Popcorn

- ½ cup unpopped popcorn
- 3 tablespoons cooking oil
- ¼ cup butter *or* margarine, melted
- 1 1½-ounce envelope cheese sauce mix

Pop the corn in hot oil according to the package directions. Place the popped corn in a large mixing bowl. Pour the melted butter or margarine over the warm popcorn; toss to coat. Add dry cheese sauce mix; toss again. Makes about 3 quarts.

Rudolph's Antlers

Shape the chocolate-covered chow mein noodles to look like reindeer antlers. There's no mistaking the red cherries for Rudolph's nose.

- 1 6-ounce package (1 cup) semisweet chocolate pieces
- ½ of a 6-ounce package (½ cup) butterscotch pieces
- 1 3-ounce can (2 cups) chow mein noodles
- 12 maraschino cherries, halved

In a medium saucepan melt chocolate and butterscotch pieces over low heat, stirring occasionally. Remove from the heat. Stir in chow mein noodles. Drop by rounded teaspoonfuls onto a waxed-paper-lined baking sheet, making V-shape cookies about 2 inches long. Place a cherry half in the center of each. Chill in the refrigerator for 1 to 2 hours or till firm. Makes 24 cookies.

Buttermilk Pralines

So smooth, they'll melt in your mouth!

2 cups packed dark brown
   sugar
1 cup buttermilk
¼ teaspoon salt
¼ cup butter *or* margarine
1 teaspoon vanilla
2 cups pecan halves *or* pieces

In a heavy 3-quart saucepan stir together the sugar, buttermilk, and salt. Bring to boiling, stirring constantly. Cook and stir over medium heat till the candy thermometer registers 234° (soft-ball stage), stirring as necessary to prevent the mixture from sticking to the pan, about 10 minutes. Remove from the heat.

Add the butter or margarine and vanilla. *Do not stir.* Cool about 30 minutes, without stirring, to 150°. Quickly stir in pecans. Beat candy for 3 minutes or till slightly thickened and glossy. Drop candy by tablespoonfuls onto a baking sheet lined with waxed paper. If candy becomes too stiff to drop, add a little hot water to make it the right consistency. Let the candy stand till cool. Makes about 30.

Crème de Menthe Squares

1¼ cups butter *or* margarine
½ cup unsweetened cocoa
   powder
3½ cups sifted powdered sugar
1 beaten egg
1 teaspoon vanilla
2 cups finely crushed graham
   crackers
⅓ cup green crème de menthe
1½ cups semisweet chocolate
   pieces

In a heavy saucepan combine ½ *cup* of the butter or margarine and the cocoa powder. Cook and stir over low heat till butter is melted. Remove from the heat; stir in ½ *cup* of the powdered sugar, the egg, and vanilla. Add the graham crackers; stir till combined. Press onto the bottom of an ungreased 13x9x2-inch baking pan.

Melt ½ *cup* of the butter or margarine. In a mixer bowl combine the melted butter or margarine and crème de menthe. Gradually add the remaining powdered sugar, beating with an electric mixer till smooth. Spread over the chocolate layer. Chill in the refrigerator for 1 hour. In a heavy small saucepan combine the remaining butter or margarine and chocolate pieces. Cook and stir over low heat till melted. Spread over the crème de menthe layer. Cover and chill for 1 to 2 hours or till firm. Cut into small squares. Store in the refrigerator. Makes about 96.

Holiday Nog

5½ cups milk
1 package 4-serving-size
   instant vanilla pudding
   mix
2 tablespoons sugar
¼ teaspoon peppermint
   extract
   Crushed striped
   peppermint candy
8 striped peppermint candy
   sticks (optional)

In a blender container combine about *half* of the milk, pudding mix, sugar, and peppermint extract, then cover and blend till smooth. Pour into a large pitcher. Stir in the remaining milk. Cover and chill till serving time.

To serve, stir and pour into glasses. Sprinkle with crushed candy. If desired, serve with peppermint sticks as stirrers. Makes 8 (6-ounce) servings.

Mint Patty Shake

1 pint chocolate ice cream
½ cup milk
2 tablespoons crème de menthe *or* 6 drops mint extract
1 teaspoon vanilla
½ teaspoon ground nutmeg

In a blender container combine the chocolate ice cream, milk, crème de menthe or mint extract, vanilla, and nutmeg. Cover; blend till mixed. If necessary, add more milk for the desired consistency. Serve immediately. Makes 4 (5-ounce) servings.

Lemon-Apricot Slush

1 cup water
2 tablespoons instant tea powder
3 12-ounce cans apricot nectar (4½ cups)
½ of a 6-ounce can frozen lemonade concentrate
1 10-ounce bottle ginger ale
¾ cup bourbon (optional)

Combine the water and instant tea powder. Stir in apricot nectar and lemonade concentrate. Stir in the ginger ale and bourbon, if desired. Pour into a shallow freezer container. Cover; seal, label, and freeze. Before serving, let frozen mixture stand at room temperature for 30 to 45 minutes or till partially thawed. Stir and spoon into serving glasses. If made without bourbon, stir additional ginger ale into each serving. Makes 12 (5-ounce) servings.

Hot and Spicy Cranberry Punch

1⅓ cups water
1 6-ounce can frozen cranberry juice concentrate
3 tablespoons honey
8 inches stick cinnamon, broken
6 whole cloves
4 cardamom pods, opened
2 cups dry red wine
1 cup cranberry liqueur *or* crème de cassis (optional)

Heat the water, cranberry juice concentrate, honey, cinnamon, cloves, and cardamom to boiling. Reduce the heat; cover and simmer for 10 minutes. Strain spices. Stir in wine and cranberry liqueur or crème de cassis, if desired. Heat through; *do not* boil. Serve in mugs. Garnish with additional stick cinnamon, if desired. Makes 8 (5-ounce) servings.

Banana-Berry Fizz

1 10-ounce package frozen sweetened strawberries, partially thawed
½ cup orange juice
1 banana, cut up
1 10-ounce bottle (1¼ cups) lemon-lime carbonated beverage
½ cup vodka (optional)

In a blender container place strawberries, orange juice, and banana. Cover and blend till smooth. Stir in carbonated beverage. Stir in vodka, if desired. Pour into glasses. Garnish each with a whole strawberry, if desired. Serve at once. Makes 6 (5-ounce) servings.

Champagne Party Punch

1 750-milliliter bottle sauterne, chilled
½ cup cognac *or* brandy, chilled
3 750-milliliter bottles champagne, chilled
1 28-ounce bottle carbonated water, chilled

Combine sauterne and cognac in a large bowl. Resting bottles on rim of the bowl, carefully pour in champagne and carbonated water. Serve in champagne glasses or punch cups. Makes about 30 (5-ounce) servings.

Make-an-Ornament Cookies

Moms and dads, here's an idea to keep the little elves
at your house busy decorating the Christmas tree
with cookies! Make the cookies ahead of time, and then
help the kids use frosting to attach various
decorations for festive homemade tree trims.

Pictured on pages 194 and 195.

2¼ cups all-purpose flour
2 teaspoons baking
   powder
½ teaspoon ground
   nutmeg (optional)
½ cup butter *or*
   margarine
1 cup sugar
1 egg
2 tablespoons milk
½ teaspoon vanilla
   Assorted decorations
   (colored sugar,
   small multicolored
   decorative candies,
   and/or crushed
   hard candies)
   Narrow ribbon
   Butter Frosting
   Food color (optional)

1 In a small mixing bowl stir together flour, baking powder, and, if desired, nutmeg. Set flour mixture aside. In a large mixer bowl beat butter or margarine with an electric mixer on medium speed about 30 seconds or till softened. Add sugar and beat till fluffy.

2 Add egg, milk, and vanilla. Beat well. Gradually add flour mixture and beat till combined. Cover and chill the dough about 1 hour.

3 Roll out dough, half at a time, on a lightly floured surface to about ¼-inch thickness. Cut into desired shapes with cookie cutters or knife, rerolling dough as necessary. Transfer cookies to ungreased cookie sheets. With a plastic drinking straw, make one hole at the top of each cookie.

4 Bake in a 375° oven for 8 to 10 minutes or till cookies are light brown around the edges. If necessary, reopen holes with a toothpick while cookies are hot. Remove cookies from the sheet to a wire rack, then cool completely.

5 Put assorted decorations in individual small plastic bowls. Tie a small piece of ribbon in the hole of each cookie for hanging. Let the children decorate the cookies by attaching the decorations to the cookies with some frosting. Let the cookies stand about 30 minutes or till the frosting is slightly dry. Makes 36 cookies.

Christmas Eve Buffet

Of all the joys of the
holiday season, one of the
sweetest is the anticipation
of the festivity and
fellowship to come. Share
the joy and anticipation
of Christmas Eve
with friends and family by
serving a buffet supper.

Serve an intimate Christmas Eve
Buffet featuring *Creamy Oyster-
Broccoli Stew* (see recipe, page
206), a *Christmas Wreath* made of
bread (see recipe, page 208),
Fluffy Cranberry-Cheese Pie (see
recipe, page 212), and *Dill Relish
Tray* (see recipe, page 210).

Creamy Oyster-Broccoli Stew

Pictured on pages 204 and 205.

3 cups milk
2 11-ounce cans condensed
cheddar cheese soup
1 10-ounce package frozen
chopped broccoli
1 cup frozen loose-pack hash
brown potatoes
1 small onion, chopped
1 pint shucked oysters *or* two
8-ounce cans whole
oysters

For soup, in a 3-quart saucepan combine the milk and the soup. Stir in the broccoli, potatoes, and onion. Cook, stirring occasionally, over medium heat till bubbly, breaking up the broccoli with a fork till thawed. Simmer, covered, for 10 minutes. Remove from the heat; cool. Cover and chill.

At serving time, in a 3-quart saucepan reheat the soup. In another saucepan cook the fresh *undrained* oysters over medium heat till edges curl. Add to soup; heat through. (If using canned oysters, just add the *undrained* oysters directly to the soup; heat through.) Makes 4 to 6 servings.

Deep-Dish Spinach-Cheese Pie

The cheese oozes out when you cut it.

2 to 2½ cups whole wheat
flour
1 package active dry yeast
¼ cup grated Parmesan
cheese
⅔ cup warm water (115° to
120°)
1 egg
4 teaspoons cooking oil
1 10-ounce package frozen
chopped spinach
2 slightly beaten eggs
1 cup ricotta cheese
1 cup shredded mozzarella
cheese (4 ounces)
½ cup shredded provolone
cheese (2 ounces)
¼ cup grated Parmesan
cheese
¼ cup fine dry bread crumbs
¼ teaspoon ground nutmeg
⅛ teaspoon pepper
1 cup chopped salami
Sprig fresh rosemary
(optional)

In a large mixer bowl combine *1 cup* of the flour, yeast, and ¼ cup Parmesan cheese. Stir in water, 1 egg, and oil. Beat with an electric mixer on low speed for ½ minute, scraping the bowl constantly. Beat for 3 minutes on high speed. Stir in as much of the remaining flour as you can with a spoon. Turn out onto a lightly floured surface. Knead in enough of the remaining flour to make a moderately stiff dough that is smooth and elastic (6 to 8 minutes). Place dough in a greased bowl; turn once. Cover; let the dough rise in a warm place till it is double (about 45 minutes).

Cook the spinach according to the package directions; drain well. Combine the 2 eggs, ricotta cheese, shredded mozzarella cheese, provolone cheese, ¼ cup Parmesan cheese, bread crumbs, nutmeg, and pepper. Stir in spinach and salami.

Punch dough down. Cover and let rest for 10 minutes. Roll out ¾ of the dough into a 13-inch circle. Place in a greased 9½-inch springform pan. Spoon the spinach mixture into the dough-lined pan. Roll out the remaining dough into a 9-inch circle. Place atop the spinach mixture; fold excess bottom dough over the top. Flute edge. Prick top in several places. Bake in a 350° oven for 45 to 50 minutes or till the pizza is done. Let stand for 5 minutes. Garnish with a sprig of fresh rosemary, if desired. Makes 8 servings.

Chicken-Vegetable Burgoo

You can do most of the preparation for this soup the day before.

8 cups water
1 5- to 5½-pound stewing chicken, cut up
1 medium onion, cut into wedges
3 stalks celery, cut up
2 bay leaves
2 cloves garlic, halved
1 teaspoon salt
¼ teaspoon pepper
3 medium carrots, thinly bias sliced
1 medium onion, chopped (½ cup)
2 tablespoons instant chicken bouillon granules
2 teaspoons dried marjoram, crushed
2 cups sliced fresh mushrooms
1 small zucchini, thinly sliced
1 10-ounce package frozen peas

In a Dutch oven or large kettle combine the water, chicken, onion wedges, celery, bay leaves, garlic, salt, and pepper. Bring to boiling; reduce the heat. Simmer, covered, for 2 hours or till chicken is tender. Remove chicken from the broth; set aside. Strain broth, discarding vegetables; skim off fat. Return the broth to the Dutch oven or kettle. Stir in the carrots, chopped onion, bouillon granules, and marjoram. Simmer, covered, for 15 minutes or till carrots are crisp-tender.

Meanwhile, when the chicken is cool enough to handle, remove and discard skin and bones. Cut chicken into 1-inch pieces; add to broth. Cover and chill the chicken mixture for up to 24 hours.

In a Dutch oven or large kettle reheat the chicken mixture, covered, for 30 minutes, stirring occasionally. Stir sliced mushrooms, zucchini, and peas into the chicken mixture. Cover and simmer for 10 to 15 minutes more or till vegetables are tender, stirring occasionally. Makes 8 to 10 servings.

Onion Biscuit Rounds

2 cups packaged biscuit mix
⅔ cup light cream
⅓ cup finely chopped onion
2 tablespoons butter or margarine
  Sesame seed or poppy seed

Place the biscuit mix in a mixing bowl; add cream. Stir just till dough clings together. Knead the dough gently on a lightly floured surface for 10 to 12 strokes. Roll dough to a ¼-inch thickness. Cut with a 1½-inch biscuit cutter, dipping the cutter into flour between cuts. Place on an ungreased baking sheet. Press an indentation about 1½ inches in diameter in the center of each.

Cook the onion in butter or margarine till tender. Place *1 teaspoon* of the onion mixture into *each* indentation. Sprinkle biscuit edges with sesame seed or poppy seed. Bake in a 425° oven for 10 to 12 minutes or till done. Serve warm. Makes 10 to 12 biscuits.

Herb Biscuit Spirals

2 cups all-purpose flour
1 tablespoon baking powder
2 teaspoons sugar
½ cup butter or margarine
1 beaten egg
1 8-ounce carton dairy sour cream
2 tablespoons milk
1 tablespoon butter or margarine, melted
2 tablespoons grated Parmesan cheese
¼ teaspoon dried dillweed

In a mixing bowl stir together flour, baking powder, and sugar. Cut in the ½ cup butter or margarine till the mixture resembles coarse crumbs. Make a well in the center. In a small mixing bowl combine egg, sour cream, and milk; add all at once to dry mixture. Stir just till dough clings together. Turn out onto a lightly floured surface; knead gently for 12 to 15 strokes.

Roll dough into a 15x8-inch rectangle. Brush with the 1 tablespoon melted butter or margarine. Combine Parmesan cheese and dillweed. Sprinkle atop the dough. Fold dough lengthwise to make a 15x4-inch rectangle. Cut into fifteen 1x4-inch strips.

Holding a strip at both ends, twist in opposite directions twice, forming a spiral. Repeat with the remaining strips. Place on a lightly greased baking sheet, pressing both of the ends down. Bake in a 450° oven about 10 minutes or till the biscuit spirals are done. Serve warm. Makes 15 spirals.

Christmas Wreath

Pictured on pages 204 and 205.

2¼ to 2¾ cups all-purpose
    flour
  1 package active dry yeast
  ¾ cup milk
  3 tablespoons sugar
  3 tablespoons butter *or*
    margarine
  ¼ teaspoon salt
  1 egg
    Milk
    Pecan halves

In a large mixer bowl combine *1 cup* of the flour and the yeast. Heat milk, sugar, butter or margarine, and salt just till warm (115° to 120°) and butter starts to melt, stirring constantly. Add to flour mixture; add egg. Beat with an electric mixer on low speed for ½ minute, scraping bowl constantly. Beat for 3 minutes at high speed. Stir in as much of the remaining flour as you can mix in with a spoon. Turn out onto a lightly floured surface. Knead in enough of the remaining flour to make a moderately soft dough that is smooth and elastic (3 to 5 minutes total). Place in a lightly greased bowl; turn once to grease the surface. Cover; let rise till double (about 1 hour).

Punch dough down; divide into 3 portions and shape each into a ball. Cover; let rest 10 minutes. Roll each ball into a 20-inch rope. Grease the outside of a 6-ounce custard cup and invert the dish in the center of a greased baking sheet. Starting at the center, braid ropes loosely to the ends. Wrap braid around custard cup, stretching as necessary to join ends; pinch to seal. Cover; let rise till nearly double (about 30 minutes).

Brush carefully with milk; tuck pecan halves into braid. Bake in a 375° oven about 20 minutes or till done. Cool bread on a wire rack. Loosen braid from the custard cup with a narrow spatula; remove the cup. If desired, wrap, seal, label, and freeze bread till needed. To thaw, let stand at room temperature. Makes 1 wreath.

Carrot-Zucchini Salad

An easy salad to put together.

  4 lettuce leaves
1¼ cups shredded unpeeled
    zucchini
1¼ cups shredded carrots
  ¼ cup alfalfa sprouts
  2 to 3 tablespoons oil-and-
    vinegar salad dressing
    Carrot flowers (optional)

Line 4 salad plates with lettuce leaves. Layer the shredded zucchini and the shredded carrots on the salad plates. Top with the alfalfa sprouts. Pass the oil-and-vinegar salad dressing to drizzle over the salads. If desired, garnish each salad with a carrot flower made with paper-thin slices of carrot. Makes 4 servings.

Squash-Stuffed Baked Apples

  8 medium baking apples
  ½ cup packed brown sugar
  ½ cup orange juice
  ½ cup water
  2 tablespoons butter *or*
    margarine
  1 12-ounce package frozen
    mashed cooked winter
    squash
  1 tablespoon brown sugar
  ¼ teaspoon salt
  ¼ teaspoon ground nutmeg

Core apples and peel ¼ of the way down; trim bottoms to stand upright. Scoop out the apple centers, leaving a ½-inch-thick shell. Chop removed apple; set aside. Place apples in a 13x9x2-inch baking dish. Combine the ½ cup brown sugar, orange juice, and water. Pour over the apples. Bake, uncovered, in a 325° oven about 50 minutes or till nearly tender.

Meanwhile, in a saucepan cook the chopped apple in butter or margarine for 2 to 3 minutes. Add squash. Cover and cook over low heat for 15 minutes, stirring frequently. Stir in the 1 tablespoon brown sugar, the salt, and nutmeg. Remove apples from oven. Spoon squash mixture into apple shells. Sprinkle filling with additional ground nutmeg, if desired. Return to the 325° oven and bake about 30 minutes or till heated through. Transfer to a serving platter; drizzle pan juices over apples. Makes 8 servings.

Share a German Christmas
tradition—*Squash-Stuffed Baked
Apples* sprinkled with nutmeg.

Dill Relish Tray

Pictured on pages 204 and 205.

2 cups cauliflower flowerets
    or one 10-ounce package
    frozen cauliflower
1 pound carrots, cut into
    1-inch pieces, *or* one
    16-ounce can whole
    carrots, drained
1 small onion, sliced and
    separated into rings
½ cup Italian salad dressing
½ teaspoon dried dillweed
1 bunch radishes
1 8-ounce can jellied
    cranberry sauce, chilled

Cook the fresh cauliflower and fresh carrots separately in boiling unsalted water for 10 minutes; drain. (Or, cook the frozen cauliflower according to the package directions; drain. Cut large pieces in half. Drain canned carrots.) Place the cauliflower, carrots, and onion in a shallow dish. In a screwtop jar shake together Italian dressing and dillweed. Pour over vegetables. Cover; marinate for several hours, spooning marinade over the vegetables several times. Meanwhile, cut the radishes to resemble chrysanthemums; chill in ice water for several hours.

Before serving, arrange vegetables, radishes, and slices of the jellied cranberry sauce on a serving tray. Garnish with some celery leaves and parsley sprigs, if desired. Makes 4 to 6 servings.

Mexican Christmas Salad

2 cups peeled, sliced jicama
1 20-ounce can pineapple
    chunks
1 8-ounce can julienne beets
1 tablespoon lemon juice
1 to 2 teaspoons aniseed
¼ teaspoon salt
    Shredded lettuce
2 bananas
2 large oranges, peeled and
    sectioned
¼ cup peanuts
2 tablespoons pomegranate
    seeds
½ cup mayonnaise *or* salad
    dressing

In a large bowl combine the jicama, *undrained* pineapple, and *undrained* beets. Stir in lemon juice, aniseed, and salt. Cover and chill for several hours, gently stirring once or twice.

Drain the beet mixture, reserving 2 tablespoons of the liquid. Line a serving platter with shredded lettuce. Arrange beets, pineapple, and jicama atop the lettuce. Slice the bananas; arrange banana slices and orange sections on the platter. Sprinkle the peanuts and pomegranate seeds over the salad. In a bowl stir together mayonnaise or salad dressing and the 2 tablespoons reserved beet liquid; pass dressing to spoon atop the salad. Makes 10 servings.

Mincemeat Fruitcake

2 cups prepared mincemeat
2 cups diced mixed candied
    fruits and peels
1 cup chopped walnuts
¾ cup packed brown sugar
¼ cup butter *or* margarine
2 eggs
1 teaspoon vanilla
2½ cups all-purpose flour
½ teaspoon baking powder
½ teaspoon baking soda
¼ teaspoon salt
¼ cup brandy *or* bourbon
    Brandy Icing
    Candied fruit (optional)

Stir together mincemeat, candied fruits and peels, and nuts. In a large mixer bowl beat the brown sugar and butter or margarine till fluffy. Add eggs and vanilla; mix well. Thoroughly stir together flour, baking powder, soda, and salt. Stir into the sugar mixture. (Batter will be stiff.) Stir in fruit mixture. Turn into a greased and floured 12-cup fluted tube pan or 10-inch tube pan. Bake in a 325° oven for 65 minutes or till done. Cool; remove from the pan. Wrap in a brandy-soaked cheesecloth. Overwrap with foil. Store in a cool place for at least 1 week before serving. To serve, drizzle with Brandy Icing. Garnish with candied fruit, if desired. Slice thinly to serve. Makes 1 cake.

BRANDY ICING: Add 1 tablespoon *brandy or bourbon* and ½ teaspoon *vanilla* to 1 cup sifted *powdered sugar*. Add *milk* till the mixture is of drizzling consistency (1 to 2 tablespoons).

Cranberry-Pecan Tarts

2 cups all-purpose flour
½ teaspoon salt
⅔ cup shortening
6 to 7 tablespoons cold water
3 eggs
1 cup light corn syrup
⅔ cup sugar
Dash salt
⅓ cup butter *or* margarine
1¼ cups fresh cranberries
1¼ cups broken pecans

In a bowl stir together flour and the ½ teaspoon salt. Cut in the shortening till pieces are the size of small peas. Sprinkle water over the mixture, 1 tablespoon at a time, tossing gently with a fork till all is moistened. Form into a ball. Divide into 12 portions. On a floured surface roll each into a 6-inch circle. Fit circles into 12 fluted 4-inch tart pans, pinching to make pleats at intervals to fit the dough into the pans.

In a bowl beat eggs slightly; add corn syrup, sugar, and the dash salt. Stir till sugar is dissolved. Add melted butter or margarine; mix well. Stir in cranberries and pecans. Divide the mixture among the pastry-lined tart pans on a baking sheet. Bake in a 350° oven for 30 to 35 minutes or till the filling is set. Cool thoroughly on a wire rack; remove from the tart pans. Makes 12 servings.

Desserts from Christmases Past

Cranberries

Cranberries have been a holiday mainstay since the Indians told the Pilgrims that those wild red berries in the marshes near Plymouth were good to eat.

The Irish named them "bogberries" after seeing cranes eat the fruit as they waded through the marshy bogs where the berries grew. The English called them "craneberries" because the unopened flower and corolla looked like a crane's head and neck.

Cranberries first appeared on the table as a sauce, but later were used in pies, tarts, breads, and jellies.

Mincemeat

No one knows when Little Jack Horner sat down in his corner to eat that Christmas pie. But we do know it was a mince pie he was nibbling on. A Christmas favorite for 500 years, mince pie originally was made with chopped partridges, pheasants, hares, and later, chopped beef. Still later, cooks added suet, sugar, apples, molasses, raisins, currants, and spices. The pie originally had an oblong shape and its lattice crust symbolized the Bethlehem manger filled with hay. Apples stood for growth; spices represented the Wise Men's gifts.

Fruitcakes

Once called the "great cake," fruitcakes are usually oblong and individually cooked for each person. In the South, cooks were known to compete for the blackest cake. Some even browned the flour before mixing to darken the color.

Fluffy Cranberry-Cheese Pie

Pictured on page 205.

1 3-ounce package raspberry-
    or cranberry-orange-
    flavored gelatin
⅓ cup sugar
1¼ cups cranberry juice
    cocktail
1 cup fresh cranberries,
    ground
1 3-ounce package cream
    cheese, softened
¼ cup sugar
1 tablespoon milk
1 teaspoon vanilla
½ cup whipping cream
1 9-inch baked and cooled
    pastry shell

In a bowl combine gelatin and the ⅓ cup sugar. Bring the cranberry juice to boiling; pour over the gelatin mixture, stirring to dissolve. Stir in the ground cranberries. Chill till mixture is the consistency of unbeaten egg whites. Meanwhile, in a small mixer bowl beat cream cheese, the ¼ cup sugar, the milk, and vanilla till fluffy. Beat cream just to soft peaks; fold into the cheese mixture. Wash beaters. Place cranberry mixture in a bowl of ice water. Using clean beaters, beat till fluffy. If necessary, let stand till mixture mounds. Spread cream cheese mixture over the bottom of the pastry shell. Top with cranberry mixture. Chill for several hours or overnight. Store, covered, in the refrigerator till needed. If desired, pipe additional whipped cream atop; garnish with cranberries. Makes 1 pie.

Cassata Rum Cake

6 slightly beaten eggs
1 cup sugar
1 cup all-purpose flour
¼ cup unsalted butter, melted
    and cooled
3 tablespoons Crème de
    Noya *or* almond liqueur
3 tablespoons light rum
2 cups whipping cream
1 tablespoon powdered sugar
¼ teaspoon vanilla
1 ounce (1 square) semisweet
    chocolate, grated
⅔ cup toasted almonds, finely
    chopped
½ cup ricotta cheese, sieved
    (3 ounces)
¼ teaspoon ground cinnamon
⅛ teaspoon ground nutmeg
    Additional whipped cream
    (optional)
    Chocolate-dipped almonds
    (optional)

Butter and flour the bottom and sides of an 8-inch springform pan; set aside. In a large mixer bowl combine eggs and sugar. Place bowl over a large saucepan of hot water (water should not touch bottom of the bowl and should not boil); heat over low heat, stirring frequently, about 5 minutes or till lukewarm. Remove from the heat; beat egg mixture with an electric mixer on high speed about 10 to 12 minutes or till mixture is thick and more than double in volume. Sprinkle flour about one-third at a time over egg mixture; fold in gently. Fold in butter. Pour batter into prepared pan. Bake in a 350° oven about 40 minutes. Let cool for 10 minutes. Remove from pan; cool on a wire rack.

Combine liqueur and rum; set aside. Cut cake horizontally into 3 layers. (For easier slicing, place cooled cake in the freezer about 25 minutes before cutting.) In a large mixer bowl combine whipping cream, powdered sugar, and vanilla. Beat till soft peaks form. Place first layer of cake on a serving plate; brush generously with liqueur mixture. Top with one-fourth of the whipped cream. Sprinkle with a generous tablespoon of grated chocolate and a generous tablespoon of chopped almonds. Repeat. Top with remaining cake layer.

To the remaining whipped cream mixture, add ricotta cheese, cinnamon, and nutmeg. Frost top and sides of cake with ricotta mixture. Sprinkle remaining chocolate over top. Press remaining almonds into ricotta mixture on sides. Chill for several hours or overnight. Garnish base with small rosettes of whipped cream and some chocolate-dipped almonds, if desired. Makes 12 to 16 servings.

Light Wassail Bowl

1 large orange, halved
15 whole cloves
9 inches stick cinnamon, broken up
¾ teaspoon whole allspice, crushed
3 750-milliliter bottles (about 9 cups) light Burgundy
¾ cup brandy
½ cup packed brown sugar

Stud the orange halves with the cloves. Wrap and tie cinnamon and allspice in a cheesecloth bag. In a Dutch oven combine the orange halves, spice bag, Burgundy, brandy, and brown sugar. Cover; simmer for 15 minutes. Transfer to a heat-proof punch bowl. Discard the spice bag. Float orange halves atop. Makes 9 cups.

Spicy Coffee Brew

2 cups ground coffee
9 inches stick cinnamon, broken
6 whole cloves
1 vanilla bean, split lengthwise and cut up

Stir together the ground coffee, stick cinnamon, whole cloves, and vanilla bean. Store in a tightly covered container in the refrigerator for at least 2 weeks.

Stir the mix before using. To use, for *each* serving, measure *1 tablespoon* of the coffee mix into a coffee maker basket and add ¾ cup *cold water.* Prepare drip or percolator coffee according to the manufacturer's directions. Pour the coffee into heat-proof glasses or cups. Makes enough for 32 (6-ounce) servings.

Irish Coffee

6 cups hot strong coffee
1 cup Irish whiskey *or* bourbon
¼ cup packed brown sugar
½ cup whipping cream, whipped

In a coffeepot or heat-proof decanter combine coffee, whiskey or bourbon, and sugar. Stir to dissolve sugar. To serve, pour into heat-proof mugs; top with the whipped cream. Makes 8 (6-ounce) servings.

Citrus Punch

2 cups cold water
1 6-ounce can grapefruit juice, chilled
⅓ cup sugar-sweetened lemonade mix
2 tablespoons grenadine syrup
Ice cubes

In a pitcher or bowl combine cold water, grapefruit juice, lemonade mix, and grenadine syrup; stir till mix is dissolved. To serve, fill 3 tall glasses with ice cubes, then pour in the grapefruit juice mixture. Makes 3 (8-ounce) servings.

Eat, drink, and be merry by serving *Light Wassail Bowl* and whipped-cream-topped *Irish Coffee.*

213

Skating Party

When the sky is clear and the air is brisk, gather some friends for an outdoor skating party. After the invigorating fun, invite everyone in by the fire for these simple-to-make, warm-me-up-quick appetite pleasers.

Hot and Hearty Sausage Soup

2 pounds Italian sausage links
2 cups dry white wine
2 cloves garlic, minced
1 medium onion, finely chopped (½ cup)
5 cups chopped cabbage
1 28-ounce can tomatoes, cut up
1 cup water
1 4-ounce can green chili peppers, rinsed, seeded, and chopped

Using a fork, prick the sausage several times. Cut into 1-inch pieces; place in a large mixing bowl. Stir in wine and garlic. Marinate for 30 minutes.

Drain the sausage pieces, reserving the marinade. In a Dutch oven or large kettle cook the sausage pieces and onion till the meat is brown and the onion is tender. Drain off fat. Stir in the reserved marinade. Bring to boiling; reduce the heat. Cover and simmer for 20 minutes.

Stir the chopped cabbage, *undrained* tomatoes, water, and green chili peppers into the sausage mixture. Return to boiling; reduce the heat. Cover and simmer for 20 minutes more, stirring occasionally. (For reheating later, cool and chill the soup at this point.*) Makes 8 to 10 servings.

*NOTE: To reheat the chilled soup, place it in a Dutch oven or large kettle; cover and bring to boiling (about 30 minutes), stirring occasionally. If the soup is too thick, stir in an additional 1 cup *water* and heat through.

Country-Style Bean Chili

2 medium onions, sliced and separated into rings
1 large green pepper, cut into strips and halved crosswise
1 tablespoon cooking oil
2 15½-ounce cans red kidney beans, drained
2 15½-ounce cans garbanzo beans, drained
2 14½-ounce cans chicken broth
2 12-ounce cans beer
1 16-ounce can refried beans
1 tablespoon paprika
1 tablespoon chili powder
1 tablespoon prepared mustard
1 tablespoon chopped canned green chili peppers
½ teaspoon dried basil, crushed
½ teaspoon dried oregano, crushed
Croutons
2 cups shredded cheddar cheese (8 ounces)

In a Dutch oven cook onion and green pepper in oil till tender. Stir in kidney beans, garbanzo beans, broth, beer, refried beans, paprika, chili powder, mustard, chili peppers, basil, and oregano. Bring to boiling; reduce the heat. Cover; simmer for 1 hour, stirring occasionally. (For reheating later, cool and chill soup at this point.*) Serve with croutons and cheese. Makes 8 to 10 servings.

*NOTE: To reheat soup, cover and bring to boiling (about 45 minutes), stirring occasionally. Serve with croutons and cheese.

Curried Cheese Spread

1 8-ounce carton dairy sour cream
1 3-ounce package cream cheese, softened
¼ cup finely chopped pimiento-stuffed olives
¼ cup finely chopped celery
2 tablespoons finely chopped green pepper
1 tablespoon finely chopped green onion
1 tablespoon lemon juice
2 teaspoons curry powder
¼ teaspoon Worcestershire sauce
  Dash bottled hot pepper sauce
⅓ cup finely crushed rich round crackers
1 tablespoon butter *or* margarine, melted
  Sliced pimiento-stuffed olives
  Assorted crackers *or* vegetable dippers

Line a 3-cup mold or bowl with clear plastic wrap; set aside. Combine sour cream, cream cheese, ¼ cup olives, celery, green pepper, onion, lemon juice, curry powder, Worcestershire sauce, and hot pepper sauce. Combine ⅓ cup crushed crackers and butter.

Spoon about *one-third* of the sour cream mixture into the mold; sprinkle with *half* of the crumb mixture. Repeat the layers, ending with the sour cream mixture. Cover and chill for at least 4 hours.

Unmold onto a plate; remove the plastic wrap. Garnish with olive slices. Serve with crackers or dippers. Makes 1⅔ cups.

Fruit and Orange Dip

1 8-ounce package cream cheese, cut up
1 7-ounce jar marshmallow creme
2 teaspoons finely shredded orange peel
2 tablespoons orange juice
½ cup broken walnuts
3 medium apples, cut into wedges
  Lemon juice
1 11-ounce can mandarin orange sections, drained

In a small mixer bowl beat together the cream cheese, marshmallow creme, orange peel, and juice. Fold in walnuts. Brush apple wedges with lemon juice. Alternately thread apples and oranges onto toothpicks. Serve with cheese mixture. Makes 2 cups.

Ham Crescents

Make these ahead of time and refrigerate till you're ready to pop them in the oven.

¾ pound ground fully cooked ham
½ cup meatless spaghetti sauce
¼ cup chopped green pepper
2 packages (8 rolls each) refrigerated crescent rolls
  Plain yogurt (optional)

Stir together ham, spaghetti sauce, and green pepper. Separate crescent rolls into 16 triangles. At wide end of *each,* place about *3 tablespoons* of the ham mixture.

Roll up, starting at the wide end. Arrange rolls on a greased baking sheet. Cover and chill in the refrigerator for up to 2 hours.

Before serving, bake the filled rolls in a 375° oven for 25 to 30 minutes or till the tops are golden brown. Let cool for 10 minutes. Dollop with plain yogurt, if desired. Makes 16 appetizers.

Party Scramble

Make extra and give it away.

3 cups bite-size shredded
  wheat biscuits
2 cups salted mixed nuts
1½ cups round toasted oat
  cereal
1½ cups bite-size shredded
  wheat squares *or* bite-size
  shredded corn squares
2½ cups small pretzel sticks *or*
  one 3-ounce can chow
  mein noodles
½ cup butter *or* margarine
⅓ cup grated Parmesan
  cheese
1½ teaspoons chili powder
⅛ teaspoon garlic powder

In a 13x9x2-inch baking pan combine the shredded wheat biscuits, mixed nuts, toasted oat cereal, and bite-size shredded wheat or corn squares.

Bake the cereal mixture in a 300° oven about 5 minutes or till warm. Stir in the small pretzel sticks or the chow mein noodles.

Melt the butter or margarine; drizzle over the cereal mixtue. Stir together the grated Parmesan cheese, chili powder, and garlic powder; sprinkle over the cereal mixture. Stir to coat the mixture evenly. Bake in a 300° oven for 15 to 20 minutes more or till the cereal is dry and crisp, stirring twice during baking. Remove from the oven. Cool. Store in tightly covered containers or plastic bags. Makes about 10½ cups.

Nutty Caramel Corn

So good, you'll eat it by the handfuls.

20 cups popped popcorn
  (about 1 cup unpopped)
2 cups packed brown sugar
1 cup butter *or* margarine
½ cup light corn syrup
½ teaspoon salt
½ teaspoon baking soda
½ teaspoon cream of tartar
2½ cups dry roasted peanuts

Remove all the unpopped kernels from the popped popcorn. Put the popcorn in a large roasting pan and keep it warm in a 300° oven.

Butter the sides of a heavy 3-quart saucepan. In the saucepan combine the brown sugar, butter or margarine, light corn syrup, and salt. Cook over medium heat to boiling, stirring constantly with a wooden spoon to dissolve sugar. Avoid splashing the mixture on the sides of the pan. Carefully clip a candy thermometer to the side of the pan. Cook over medium heat, without stirring, till the temperature reaches 260° (hard-ball stage). This should take about 5 minutes. Remove the saucepan from the heat; remove the candy thermometer. Stir in the baking soda and cream of tartar.

Slowly pour the brown sugar mixture over the warm popcorn. Gently stir to evenly coat the popcorn. Stir in the dry roasted peanuts. Bake in a 300° oven for 30 minutes, stirring the popcorn mixture after 15 minutes. Transfer the popcorn mixture to a large shallow pan. Cool. Store in tightly covered containers or plastic bags. Makes about 20 cups.

Mocha Cinnamon Fingers

Pictured on page 218.

2 teaspoons instant coffee
  crystals
½ teaspoon water
½ teaspoon vanilla
2 cups all-purpose flour
1 teaspoon ground cinnamon
1 cup butter *or* margarine
½ cup sugar
½ cup packed brown sugar
1 egg yolk
1 6-ounce package (1 cup)
  semisweet chocolate
  pieces
1 cup finely chopped walnuts
  or pecans

In a small bowl stir together the coffee crystals, water, and vanilla till the coffee crystals are dissolved. In a medium bowl stir together the flour and cinnamon.

In a large mixer bowl beat butter or margarine till softened. Add sugar and brown sugar and beat till fluffy. Add egg yolk and coffee mixture and beat well. Gradually add flour mixture, beating till well mixed. Press the mixture evenly into an ungreased 15x10x1-inch baking pan.

Bake in a 350° oven for 15 to 18 minutes or till done. Immediately sprinkle chocolate pieces over top. Let stand till chocolate is softened, then spread evenly. Sprinkle with nuts. Cut into bars while warm. Cool. Makes 48.

Fruitcake Squares

So easy to make, but oh so good!

⅓ cup butter *or* margarine
1 12-ounce box vanilla
  wafers, finely crushed
1 cup pecan halves
¾ cup chopped dates
¾ cup halved green candied
  cherries
¾ cup halved red candied
  cherries
½ cup chopped candied
  pineapple
1 14-ounce can (1¼ cups)
  sweetened condensed milk
¼ cup bourbon *or* milk

Melt butter, then pour into a
15x10x1-inch baking pan, tilting
pan. Sprinkle vanilla wafer crumbs
evenly over butter. Arrange nuts,
dates, and candied fruits evenly
over crumbs and press down gently. Combine condensed milk and
bourbon or milk and pour over
top. Bake in a 350° oven for 20 to
25 minutes or till set. Cool. Cut
into squares. Makes 60.

Grasshopper Cheesecake Bars

1 8-ounce package cream
  cheese
¾ cup all-purpose flour
⅓ cup sugar
⅓ cup unsweetened cocoa
  powder
6 tablespoons butter *or*
  margarine
¼ cup sugar
1 egg
½ teaspoon peppermint
  extract
4 or 5 drops green food
  coloring
¼ cup milk

Place cream cheese in small mixer
bowl and let stand at room temperature about 30 minutes or till
softened. Stir together flour, ⅓
cup sugar, and cocoa powder. Cut
in butter or margarine till mixture
resembles fine crumbs. Set aside 1
cup of the mixture for topping.
Press remaining mixture onto the
bottom of an ungreased 8x8x2-
inch baking pan. Bake in a 350°
oven for 15 minutes.

Meanwhile, beat together softened cream cheese and ¼ cup sugar till fluffy. Add egg, peppermint
extract, and food coloring; beat
well. Stir in milk. Spread over
baked layer.

Sprinkle top with reserved
crumbs. Return to the 350° oven
and bake for 20 to 25 minutes or
till done. Cool. Cut into bars. Chill
to store. Makes 25.

Serve festive *Mocha Cinnamon
Fingers* (see recipe, page 217),
Fruitcake Squares, and *Grasshopper
Cheesecake Bars* with mugs
of your favorite beverage.

Hot and Spicy Berry Cider

8 cups apple cider *or* apple juice
1 10-ounce package frozen unsweetened red raspberries *or* frozen unsweetened sliced strawberries
4 inches stick cinnamon
1½ teaspoons whole cloves
1 medium apple, cut into 8 wedges

In a large saucepan combine the apple cider or juice, raspberries or strawberries, stick cinnamon, and whole cloves. Bring mixture to boiling; reduce the heat. Cover and simmer for 10 minutes. Strain through a sieve lined with cheesecloth. To serve, pour the cider into 8 heat-proof glasses or cups; float an apple wedge in each. Makes 8 (8-ounce) servings.

Hot Buttered Lemonade Mix

Keep this mix frozen till you're ready to use it. Then just add boiling water.

1 cup butter *or* margarine, softened
½ cup sifted powdered sugar
½ cup sugar-sweetened lemonade mix
½ teaspoon ground cinnamon
1 pint vanilla ice cream (2 cups), softened
    Ground nutmeg (optional)

In a mixer bowl place butter, powdered sugar, lemonade mix, and cinnamon; beat with an electric mixer on low speed till combined. Add ice cream; beat just till combined. Turn into a 4-cup freezer container. Seal, label, and freeze for at least 7 hours.

To use, for *each* serving, spoon about ½ *cup* of the ice cream mixture into a mug. Add ½ cup *boiling water*. Stir to combine. If desired, lightly sprinkle ground nutmeg atop. Makes enough mix for 10 (6-ounce) servings.

Spiced Beer Toddy

Just the thing to warm you up after a chilly outdoors adventure.

8 cups water
2 12-ounce cans frozen lemonade concentrate
½ cup honey
12 inches stick cinnamon, broken
2 teaspoons whole allspice
2 teaspoons whole cloves
4 12-ounce cans beer
1 cup gin *or* vodka

In an 8-quart Dutch oven or large kettle combine the water, lemonade concentrate, and honey. For the spice bag, place cinnamon pieces, whole allspice, and whole cloves in cheesecloth and tie; add to the lemonade mixture. Bring the mixture to boiling; reduce the heat. Cover and simmer for 10 minutes. Remove spice bag; discard. Stir in beer and gin or vodka; heat through. Serve warm. Make 22 (6-ounce) servings.

Spiced Percolator Punch

Make this punch in a large percolator and let guests serve themselves right from the percolator.

3 24-ounce bottles unsweetened white grape juice
1 46-ounce can unsweetened pineapple juice
1 6-ounce can frozen lemonade concentrate, thawed
½ cup sugar
12 inches stick cinnamon, broken
4 teaspoons whole cloves
2 teaspoons whole allspice
    Peel of 1 lemon, cut into strips

In a 24-cup electric percolator combine the white grape juice, unsweetened pineapple juice, thawed lemonade concentrate, and sugar.

Place the cinnamon stick pieces, whole cloves, whole allspice, and lemon peel into the coffee maker basket. Prepare according to the manufacturer's directions. To serve, pour the punch into heat-proof glasses or cups. Makes about 32 (4-ounce) servings.

Yuletide Yummies for a Cookie Exchange

Part of the holiday fun is making lots of cookies to have for parties, gifts, and spur-of-the-moment snacks. But if you're too busy to spend hours baking, organize a cookie exchange—it'll ease your holiday time crunch and it's the perfect excuse to get together with friends.

How to Plan a Holiday Cookie Exchange

Hosting a cookie exchange for your friends or neighbors needn't add to the hustle and bustle of the season if you follow these helpful hints.

● Start by determining how many people you can include comfortably and without confusion. Four or five friends may be enough if you're a novice at organizing this kind of gathering. For a large assortment of different cookies, invite 10 or 12 people. Keep in mind, however, that the more people who are involved, the more organized you will have to be.

● Ask each participant to bring six dozen cookies.

● Set aside a long table or counter where the containers can be placed as guests arrive. (Have each guest bring an empty container to take his or her cookies home in.) To avoid confusion, all containers and lids should be marked with the owner's name.

● When all the guests have arrived, divide 72 (six dozen) by the number of participants and note next to each recipe how many of each type of cookie every guest may take. Then start a round robin, with each guest filling his or her empty container. Arrange extra cookies on a "tasting plate."

● Exchanges may be set up in conjunction with a potluck meal or as a dessert party. Try to schedule the exchange in late November or early December to give participants sufficient time to bake before the holiday rush and ensure a ready supply of cookies throughout the holidays.

● If your friends would like to share their baking secrets, ask all the participants to bring copies of their recipes.

Hazelnut Snaps

½ cup packed brown sugar
½ cup butter *or* margarine
⅓ cup corn syrup
¾ cup all-purpose flour
1 cup ground hazelnuts
2 tablespoons hazelnut-flavored liqueur *or* brandy

In a small saucepan combine sugar, butter or margarine, and corn syrup. Cook and stir over medium heat till well blended. Remove from the heat; stir in the flour, hazelnuts, and liqueur. Drop batter from a rounded teaspoon onto a greased foil-lined cookie sheet. Bake in a 350° oven for 9 to 11 minutes. Let stand for 1 minute. Remove from cookie sheet, one at a time, and shape as desired (pull up 3 sides to center to form a triangle, or roll around oiled handle of a wooden spoon). Cool on a wire rack. If cookies become too cool to shape, return to oven for 1 to 2 minutes to soften. Makes about 48 cookies.

Mincemeat Pastries

Eating one of these pastries is like eating a miniature mincemeat pie.

    2 cups all-purpose flour
    ¼ teaspoon salt
    1 cup butter *or* margarine
    1 8-ounce package cream
       cheese, softened
    ½ cup sifted powdered sugar
    1 cup prepared mincemeat
    1 tablespoon rum

In a mixing bowl stir together the all-purpose flour and salt; set aside. In a large mixer bowl beat the butter or margarine and softened cream cheese with an electric mixer on medium speed for 30 seconds. Add the sifted powdered sugar and beat till the mixture is fluffy. Stir the flour mixture into the beaten mixture. Cover and chill the dough for several hours or overnight.

On a lightly floured surface, roll out the dough to ⅛-inch thickness. Cut with a 2½-inch round cookie cutter. Place the cookies on an ungreased cookie sheet. Stir together the mincemeat and rum. Spoon *1 teaspoon* of the mincemeat mixture into the center of *each* cookie. Bring up 2 *adjacent* sides of the cookie and pinch to seal, forming a cornucopia or "bell." Bake in a 375° oven for 10 to 12 minutes or till cookies are lightly browned. Transfer the cookies to a wire rack to cool. Makes 48 cookies.

Teddy Bears, Funny Faces, And Angels

       Gingerbread Dough,
         Vanilla Dough, and/or
         Chocolate Dough (see
         recipe opposite)
       Beaten egg yolk
    1 tablespoon water
       Several drops red food
         coloring
       Sifted powdered sugar
       Milk *or* light cream
       Blue food coloring

Prepare desired dough and chill for 2 hours or overnight. Working with *half* of the dough at a time, roll out on a lightly floured surface to ⅛-inch thickness. Cut and trim as directed for the Teddy Bears, Funny Faces, and Angels. Place on ungreased cookie sheets. (Make a small hole at top of cookies if they are to be used as tree ornaments.) Using a fine paintbrush, paint the features of cookies with a mixture of egg yolk, water, and red food coloring. Bake in a 350° oven for 8 to 10 minutes or till set and light brown. (Thick cookies such as the Teddy Bears may require longer baking time.) Cool on a wire rack.

Combine powdered sugar with enough milk or light cream to make of piping consistency. Tint *half* of the icing with blue food coloring. Use blue and white icing in a pastry bag fitted with a decorative tip to decorate cookies.

TEDDY BEARS: For each teddy bear cookie, shape the dough into 1 large ball, 5 medium-size balls, 3 small balls, and 4 tiny balls. Then, on an ungreased cookie sheet flatten the large ball slightly for the teddy bear's body. Attach the 5 medium-size balls for the bear's head, arms, and legs. Place the 3 small balls on the head for the nose and ears. With a toothpick, draw the eyes and mouth. Arrange the 4 tiny balls atop ends of the legs and arms for the teddy bear's paws; trace a circle around each.

FUNNY FACES: Cut the dough with a 2½- or 3-inch round cookie cutter. For the nose, eyes, cheeks, mouth, and hair, use scraps of dough. For the nose, shape a narrow strip of dough into a ½-inch-long nose; place the dough in the center of the cookie. For eyes, with the tip of your finger make indentations on both sides of nose. For cheeks, roll small pieces of dough into balls and place below eyes. For mouth,

roll a thin strip of dough; arrange dough under the nose to form a smile or frown. For hair, fill a garlic press with dough. Squeeze out dough. Cut off; starting at top of cookies, press dough strands onto outer edge. Repeat pressing and cutting till desired amount of hair is obtained.

ANGELS: Roll the dough to ⅛-inch thickness. For each cookie, cut a 2½-inch rectangle; place each on an ungreased cookie sheet. For wings, cut out a 2-inch circle; halve the circle and attach to the body as wings. For the head, attach a ¾-inch ball. For the hair, fill a garlic press with dough. Squeeze out dough. Cut off with a sharp knife. Attach strands of dough to the head for hair. Place 2 small balls of dough next to the bottom of the body for the feet. Place 1 small ball of dough in the center of the body for a button. For the eyes and nose, make an indentation with your finger. Place the tiny balls of dough on the face for the cheeks.

Gingerbread Dough

1 cup butter *or* margarine
⅔ cup packed brown sugar
⅔ cup dark corn syrup *or* molasses
1½ teaspoons vanilla
1 beaten egg
4 cups all-purpose flour
¾ teaspoon baking soda
1½ teaspoons ground cinnamon
1 teaspoon ground ginger
½ teaspoon ground cloves

In a saucepan combine the butter or margarine, sugar, and corn syrup or molasses. Cook and stir over medium heat till butter is melted and sugar dissolves. Pour into a mixing bowl. Stir in the vanilla. Cool for 5 minutes. Add the egg; mix well. Stir together the flour, baking soda, cinnamon, ginger, and cloves. Add dry ingredients to the egg mixture; mix well. Divide dough in half. Cover; chill dough for 2 hours or overnight. Continue as directed in Teddy Bears, Funny Faces, and Angels.

VANILLA DOUGH: Prepare Gingerbread Dough as directed, *except* substitute ⅔ cup granulated *sugar* for the brown sugar and use *light* corn syrup. Omit the cinnamon, ginger, and cloves. Continue as directed.

CHOCOLATE DOUGH: Prepare the Gingerbread Dough as directed, *except* substitute ⅔ cup granulated *sugar* for the brown sugar, reduce butter or margarine to ⅔ cup, and melt 2 squares *unsweetened chocolate* with the butter mixture in the saucepan. Omit the ground cinnamon, ginger, and cloves. Continue as directed.

Apricot Foldovers

There's a brandy-soaked apricot inside.

2 6-ounce packages dried apricots
½ cup apricot brandy
1½ cups all-purpose flour
¼ cup sugar
¼ teaspoon ground allspice
¾ cup butter *or* margarine
1 beaten egg yolk
⅓ cup dairy sour cream
Apricot Brandy Icing

Soak apricots in ½ cup brandy at least 1 hour or overnight. Drain, reserving liquid. Pat apricots dry.

In a mixing bowl combine the flour, sugar, and allspice. Cut in the butter or margarine till mixture resembles fine crumbs. Combine egg yolk and sour cream; stir into the flour mixture. Cover; chill for several hours or overnight.

Divide the chilled dough into 2 equal portions. Keep each portion chilled till ready to use. On a lightly floured surface, roll out dough, half at a time, to ⅛-inch thickness. Cut with a 2½-inch fluted round cutter. Place each cookie on an ungreased cookie sheet. Place 1 apricot on one half of each cookie. Fold over other half, leaving apricot showing. Bake in a 350° oven about 12 minutes or till cookies are lightly browned. Transfer to a wire rack. Cool cookies completely. Dip half of each cookie in Apricot Brandy Icing. Makes 54 cookies.

APRICOT BRANDY ICING: In a bowl stir together 1 cup sifted *powdered sugar* and 2 to 3 tablespoons of reserved *apricot brandy* to make of drizzling consistency.

BONUS RECIPE INDEX

CREDITS:

Page 198: "Christmas Cheer
Recipe," Copyright © 1951 by
Christian Herald Association, Inc.
Used by permission.